The Mind of the Horse

The Mind
of the Horse

R. H. SMYTHE
M.R.C.V.S.

Examiner in Surgery to the
Royal College of Veterinary
Surgeons, 1937-1959

CASTLE BOOKS

Published by
CASTLE BOOKS
A Division of Book Sales, Inc.
114 Northfield Avenue, Edison, New Jersey 08837

First published in 1965 under the title "The Mind of the Horse"
by Country Life, part of Reed International Books Limited,
Michelin House, 81 Fulham Road, London SW36RB

ISBN 0-7858-0874-4

Contents

Illustrations

Introduction

There is no reason to doubt that, in its earliest days, the horse was suited mentally as well as physically to the kind of life it lived and that it was well adapted to the environment in which it existed. In all probability this state of things persisted up to the time when the horse first made practical acquaintance with man.

Today, one can only regard the modern horse, wholly dependent upon the whims of mankind, removed from its natural environment and living an entirely artificial life, as one of the most extraordinary of all the domesticated animals.

In its present role it exists almost entirely as a saddle horse of one kind or another, adapted to the purpose of carrying a human being on its back. Loaded in this fashion, and galloping, racing and jumping over high and difficult obstacles, the horse is carrying out a type of work for which it was never designed by nature – and what is even more remarkable, doing it extremely well.

The horse exhibits today an outstanding ability to adapt itself to unusual environment and circumstance. It displays not only a great versatility, but also a willingness to submit – within limits – to human domination; it exhibits a desire to co-operate with its rider and may even appear on a great many occasions to anticipate his wishes.

Later in this book an attempt will be made to discuss a few of the mental and physical handicaps the horse experiences within its modern environment so that the reader may better understand some of the difficulties with which every horse has to contend.

It may be hard for the present generation of young people –

or for that matter some of the older folk – to realise the over-whelming part the horse played in the history of mankind, right up to the early years of the 20th century. It was essential for all kinds of transport, for use in agriculture for the treat-ment of land and the production of crops, as much as for the conveyance of the individual or for sporting activities. Nobody imagined in those days that the internal combustion engine would ever attain the degree of efficiency which it has done, and certainly nobody ever visualised horseless roads so thickly packed with engine-propelled vehicles that the movement of traffic would be brought to a standstill by its own volume. No-one realised the extent to which the life of the town-dweller would be changed by the departure of the horse, or that before the lapse of a great many years this metamorphosis would bring about a continuous increase in the human mor-tality rate. In the year 1963, road deaths amounting to 6,230 have produced a state of affairs comparable only with those previously sustained during a period of warfare.

There is little doubt that the horse, like the ass, was first employed by man as a beast of burden, a pack animal that could be led at walking pace. In all probability, it carried its owner's belongings, or the produce of man's labour, slung across its back or, at a later date, packed into panniers woven from reeds or made of hides.

History informs us that the personal belongings of its owner so transported often included the less agile females of the family, not riding astride as they might do today, but seated in one or more pairs back to back on either side of the horse's rump, securely lashed together by means of leather thongs which encircled their respective waists. As the horse in those days was smaller, thicker set and less vivacious than it is now, it rarely moved at anything exceeding walking pace, and no outstanding exhibition of what has become 'the art of equita-tion' was demanded from its riders.

It was centuries later, probably, that some equestrian genius thought of the collar as the instrument by means of which the horse might be converted into a medium for traction. This coincided with the discovery of the wheel or of runners devised from tree-trunks.

By the invention of the collar this genius unwittingly introduced something which has caused more torture to horses through the ages than any other article of equine equipment with the exception of the bit, which in its infancy was a sadistic implement, and even today is sadly misused by a great many so-called horsemen.

The advantage of a well-fitted collar was that it enabled a draught horse of substantial bulk and build to lie forward in it when pulling a big load and so utilise its own weight in addition to the power it could exert by the use of its muscles.

By process of selection and breeding, strains of horses developed which were suitable for hauling, while others were better fitted for riding and for their ability to travel quickly from place to place.

Throughout the greater part of the world an increasing degree of attention became devoted to breeding better horses in much the same way that we now endeavour to produce better cars, better engines and better aeroplanes. Eventually a number of types or, as they became known, 'breeds' of horses made their appearance in various countries, all adapted to some particular kind of work or to some variety of human entertainment.

During the intervening centuries the horse continued to be regarded as the medium by which all goods were conveyed by road, and also as the sole instrument for the personal transport of all classes of humanity from prince to peasant. Most of mankind journeyed on horseback. Some individuals preferred a chariot, a wagonette, a dogcart or a buggy; for long distance travel they were compelled in many instances to ride in a stuffy coach over diabolical roads with the prospect of their vehicle becoming bogged down to the axles in some remote place, or held up by highwaymen mounted on fast horses.

In those times whatever one's station might be in life, whether one were the humble traveller, the gentleman in the coach or the 'gentleman of the road', one's joys and sorrows were shared with horses, experienced or endured in equine company.

The effect of this association between horse and man, as well as the continuous dependence of the horse upon its human companions, was that the animal not only underwent alteration in shape and size compatible with human requirements, but it also underwent great changes in temperament and in mentality. Horses which exhibited temper, vices or any objection to being exploited as the tools of humanity were eliminated. As time went on only those animals were bred from which displayed willingness to submit to the new circumstances in which they found themselves. In the resulting progeny primitive responses became dulled or were kept more or less under control, although they were never entirely lost. Man in moments of stress, or when, for any reason, his inhibitions are temporarily forgotten, is apt to revert to his original pattern of behaviour and to act in such manner as his primitive brain may direct.

When panic or lack of confidence in itself or its rider cause a horse to fall back upon its primitive impulses, it behaves precisely as man does in similar circumstances. The two animals are alike in this respect and when either casts off that thin veneer created by civilisation or domestication, each instantaneously becomes, for the moment at least, an entirely natural creature relying on inherent impulses to facilitate its chances of survival.

The motor-car developed into a practical proposition; it became a status symbol. Every horse-owner demanded a car, usually with a chauffeur to drive it. The latter was often the erstwhile groom promoted to a uniform; and as soon as the groom found himself able to drive a car and tootle a horn he lost all interest in the horse.

The first world war played a great part in this change-over from horse to motor transport and it was rapidly made plain that food formerly consumed by horses could be more profitably utilised in the production of beef, milk and eggs.

After the advent of peace in 1918, horseflesh still held for some its place in the market as a food for human consumption. People who hitherto had lived with horses, talked of horses and dreamed horses, suddenly lost all interest in them as living creatures and regarded this as a suitable moment to be rid of them, especially as their market value as food was greater than any sum obtainable for them for any other purpose.

Within a few years the only horses remaining with us in any appreciable number were those which played an essential part in various sports, more especially those which provided an incentive to gambling.

The horse as a companion, a worker and even a status symbol appeared to have had its day. Only the racehorses, the polo ponies, a moderate number of hunters and a few indigenous ponies remained, and among the latter only those which had escaped the trader in horseflesh.

And so things remained for a number of years. Another war came and went, and at its termination the horse population had reached its lowest ebb.

And then a new generation began to grow. It was the children of this generation who looked at the picture books of days gone by and were attracted by the illustrations of animals they were unfamiliar with. Foremost among these came the ponies and they stirred their childish imaginations. A live pony would be something unique and undoubtedly a desirable plaything. Also it would be expensive to keep. In this way the pony and eventually the horse became once more a status symbol. Money was more plentiful and the children of the new generation had to be indulged.

Today there are riding establishments of one kind or another everywhere, so much so that new legislation has been approved for their registration and administration. Children are encouraged to ride, and the girls have shown themselves superior to their brothers, who usually prefer a motor-cycle to anything on four feet.

There are countless shows and gymkhanas and pony clubs, all encouraging children to ride, and these have created an intense spirit of emulation. And, of course, show jumping has become a popular spectator sport.

The demand for ponies is far greater than the supply, and horse-dealing has again entered the ranks of big business. Prices have increased tenfold and the saddler and harness maker are back at work, and the manufacture of riding clothes and riding kit is now a flourishing trade.

Once again a great many people of all ages find pleasure in being among horses, and a considerable part of the population continues to ascribe their fortune or lack of fortune to the vagaries of the equine species.

Where previously the horse was a necessity it has more recently become a luxury, and as luxuries take precedence nowadays over necessities it seems that the horse is likely to remain with us. It cannot be doubted that in addition to all its other virtues, the horse has an aesthetic appeal to the people of this and a few other countries, even if in some lands it remains a beast of burden submitted to ill-treatment and outrage. Here, at home, it is still held in respect by a great many people who possess little acquaintance with it either at work or play.

And so, during the past decade the popularity of the horse, forsaken and discarded as it was by all its so-called friends, has been at least partially restored. It is unlikely that the horse will again lose a place in its association with mankind so long as it remains a sporting companion providing facilities for racing, hunting, show jumping and riding for pleasure; and for as long as it is left alone by well-intentioned busybodies whose main object is to put an end to sport of any kind in which animals play a part. They remain unaware of the fact that any success they achieve in such efforts will result in the wholesale extermination not only of our horses, but of a great deal of the wild life which makes our country interesting.

As far as the horse is concerned let us hope reason will prevail. So many of us are happy and wish to remain so, because the horse is again with us.

I

The Influence of the Past

Essentially the horse was, and still is, a gregarious animal accustomed to living as a member of a community. It becomes completely out of its element if removed from its fellows, compelled to behave as an individual deprived of leadership.

The word 'leadership' must be stressed since the horse is temperamentally incapable of functioning entirely of its own volition. Left to itself it tends to panic and make decisions inimical to its own safety.

One may ask, if this is the case, what are the special characteristics that single out any one individual as a potential leader. Among horses it is not usual, as among a pack of wolves, to engage in combat to the extent that one individual defeats all others; instead, it is generally accepted by the community that one horse, almost invariably a stallion, places himself at the front of the herd or drove of horses and stays there by virtue of general acceptance. It is probable that the qualification is based upon the influence of the individual's hormones; that the leader is a horse of outstanding masculinity, possessing courage and some sense of discrimination, or at least able to make a decision when faced by the choice between two possible means of escape, or between escape and holding one's own ground.

As this outstanding stallion probably sires most of the future progeny within the particular herd, such leadership must exert a potent influence.

That certain stallions found bloodlines carrying invaluable features such as temperamental characteristics, speed and endurance capabilities, is a fact accepted by all who study Thoroughbreds and the connection existing between pedigree and performance.

What happens when human influence breaks up the equine

community and singles out certain horses or foals to be maintained in domestication, deprived of association with other horses and compelled to function as individuals under human discipline?

One of the most remarkable equine characteristics, common to nearly all horses, is a capability, even a willingness, to transfer the allegiance and loyalty normally extended to another member of its own species to a human being and to obey orders transmitted to it through various channels.

In domestication the horse looks to the man for leadership. It is because it does so that it is possible, in a large percentage of instances, to train the horse to fulfil all the demands which humanity makes upon it.

Very few animals of any other species can adjust their behaviour in this manner. The horse can do it and so can the dog. The cat is willing to enter into a similar partnership only with a number of reservations, since the cat is able to live at the expense of mankind without necessarily fulfilling any obligations other than those which suit its own fancy. Both horse and dog will trade their freedom in exchange for board and lodging and are quite willing to fulfil their part of the bargain. But one cannot visualise any other animal doing so. Run through a whole zoological series in your mind and try to pick out an individual of any other species which would live amicably with man and help him with his work. Quite a variety of animals may exist in captivity but merely as lodgers, and although they may accept hospitality, few will do anything in return.

Nevertheless, as will be shown later, before one can get an insight into the mind of the domesticated horse, one must understand the primitive principles which constitute its background and realise that, while it may be taught to respond to human suggestion, it still carries within it the inherent compulsion to respond to various stimuli in the way that its early ancestors would have done. No amount of training or discipline will ever entirely overcome the influence of these stimuli which may be exerted on unforeseen occasions with unexpected consequences.

Apart from these odd occasions, whenever compelled by

circumstances to lead its life in close association with some human being, the horse accepts such a person as its leader and becomes responsive and sensitive to his commands which have had no meaning whatever to its ancestors. These stimuli, of human derivation, modify the behaviour of the horse to produce responses and patterns of behaviour, which would have been equally foreign to horses in their natural environment. They may be transmitted through the agency of touch – from human hands through the reins and bit, or by the pressure of human limbs upon the equine body, or by messages transmitted audibly by the human voice.

Horses appear to enjoy the kind of life in which everything is organised and in which they have no need to exercise their minds in order to obtain food and shelter. In this way they resemble those members of human society who prefer regimentation, an army life for example – or even in some instances a sojourn in prison – where everything is arranged for them and they have no need to expend energy in thought.

Most critics will retort that horses do not think, but before we go into that question it would be necessary to decide precisely what mental processes thought might entail. There might well be disagreement on that score.

The earliest specimen of the genus *Equus*, about which a great deal is known, was *Eohippus*, about the size of a tiny Shetland pony and only a little larger than a cocker spaniel. In many respects it resembled a very small hornless deer, apart from the fact that it carried three toes on each foot.

It must not be imagined that *Eohippus* was a highly intelligent animal, when compared with the modern show jumper, for example; nor did it need to be, since its wants were few and the day had not arrived when it would have to keep pace with the whims of humanity.

Contact with mankind always increases the intelligence quotient of those animals willing to submit to domestication. The reason is twofold. Only those which please man by falling in with his wishes are given opportunity to propagate their kind. The second reason is that the influence of the owner educates or conditions the animal into accepting a kind of life quite different in pattern from that which it has forsaken. Any animal sufficiently individual in temperament as to *refuse* to obey instructions, would be rejected. Those which remain with us today are descendants of the selected few.

Morotus Alatus, the Marsh horse, was a much larger animal than *Eohippus*. It flourished in the Lower Miocene Period and possessed three jointed toes on each foot, plus one shorter toe on the outer side of each limb. These toes terminated in sharp horny claws. Between the toes, the feet were probably partially webbed in order to prevent the animal from sinking into the soft mud of the marshes in which it lived. (See Fig. 1.)

Fig. 1. The author's impression of the outline of Morotus Alatus (the Marsh Horse) based on a study of its skeleton.

It must be remembered that a great variety of prehistoric animals, other than the horse, inhabited these same marshes. Some of them were of enormous size and it may have happened that the competition and overcrowding became too great to permit the more gentle species, including the horse family, to remain in this environment.

The result was that the horse migrated over a period of time from the marshes to the plains and even to the hills. Probably the transfer from one environment to another occupied many thousands of years and during that time its feet changed in character and shape in order to cope with the difference between a soft patch of marsh and the harder and often rocky surface of the plains and hills.

The foot of the horse during this period changed from the four-toed pattern to the three-toed and from the three-toed to the single-toed foot as we know it today. The horse thus became a 'soliped'.

Two of the toes gradually became reduced in size until they completely disappeared. The bones which formerly carried

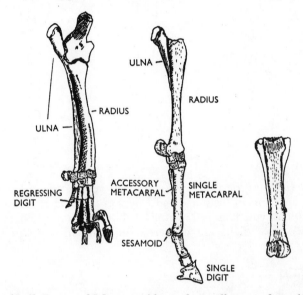

Fig. 2. (*Left*) Bones of Morotus Alatus from elbow to foot. (*Centre*) The same bones of a modern racehorse. (*Right*) Rear view of metacarpals (splint bones) of modern horse, showing the main persisting metacarpal and the two aborted metacarpals. The latter, like the aborted ulna of the modern horse, contain no medullary canals.

them dwindled away and remain as the small 'splint bones', one one either side of the cannon bone of the fore and hind limbs, still articulating with the knee and hock respectively. The fourth toe disappeared completely excepting for a small patch of horn visible on the inside of the forelimb just above the knee, known as the 'chestnut', and a similar patch on the lower and inner aspect of each hock. (See Figs. 2, 3 and 4.)

One may still wonder whether the change in the character of the foot, from the three or more toes to the single toe, made it impossible for the horse to remain on marshy ground without becoming bogged down and suffocated; or if the multiple toes proved to be unsuitable for progression on hard and rough

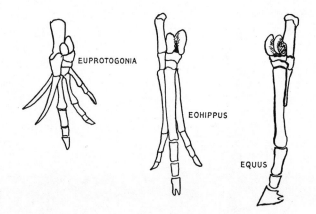

Fig. 3. (*Left and centre*) Lower bones of lower portion of hind limb of two ancestors of the horse and (*right*) of the modern horse. Note the gradual reduction in the number of bones. In the modern horse the two extra digits are converted into the small splint bones.

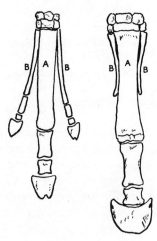

Fig. 4. (*Left*) Lower portion of limb of Protorohippus, an ancestor of the horse, compared with that of the modern animal (*right*). Note the short digit at either side, which has now shortened and fused with complete disappearance of the smaller hoofs.

surfaces, supposing that the horse was driven out of the marshes by competition with other more powerful animals.

It is probable that the change in foot structure made it easier for the horse to adapt itself to the new terrain and that the advantage lay with those animals which showed the greater tendency towards a reduction in the number of digits. Conversely, one may imagine that the change from a number of toes to the solitary toe may have represented a genetic 'mutation', that it may have come about quite suddenly in some of the foals born to normal multi-toed animals, and that as these new types tended to sink in marshy land, they had no alternative but to move on to higher and harder ground.

One might also argue that animals built on the lines of a horse might quite as well have retained three toes as one, since a great many other animals possessing a number of toes get on quite well on hard ground, have a remarkably good sense of balance and are fleet of foot.

These include the cat family and the dogs, and in fact most of the carnivorous animals.

Both the cat and the greyhound, in particular, possess great speed and the ability to turn very quickly, and they are also able to pull up to a standstill in a short space, using the pads of the feet to act as brakes and shock absorbers.

There appears to be no obvious reason why a three-toed horse should be unable to negotiate either Tattenham Corner or the Aintree jumps quite as well as one with only one prop at the lower end of each leg. Nobody could claim that the foot of the modern horse, especially when shod with iron, was in any sense skid-proof, nor has the single-toed foot any very satisfactory grip of the road surface when it comes to balancing the body on turns, or in coming to a standstill after travelling at a fast pace.

Nature, however, has endowed the soliped foot with heels, bars and a soft frog, but modern shoeing – and shoesmiths – has done a great deal to prevent these accessories from fulfilling their natural functions.

Out of all the animals which normally flourished in wild state, only a very few showed any disposition to tolerate man and live with him on the terms he desired to impose upon them.

Apart from the horse, the list of acceptors included over the course of time certain types of monkey, the dog, several kinds of ruminants, the pig, ass, elephant and camel. I have purposely omitted the cat since this animal never submits to anyone, regards itself as a being superior to any human being, and is willing to tolerate human society only for so long as it pleases, provided always it is well-fed and warmly housed.

Cattle, and farm animals generally, are in a class by themselves since they are propagated by humanity for its own purpose. They are forced to accept the hospitality of their 'owners' for so long as they yield produce; or they may be maintained only until they are in a fit condition to yield up their flesh for human consumption. A great many of them, ranging from bovines to poultry, are now bred to such a standard that their life on earth is a very short one, endured under conditions which render its shortness a cause for thankfulness. Fortunately, horses have never been bred especially for the purpose of satisfying human appetites, although in a great many countries, including our own especially during recent years, the flesh of the horse has been regularly eaten, usually after the animal could serve no other useful purpose.

One of the first things any young horse has to do after getting over its initial shyness in human society is to learn to accept the human being seated upon its back as a partner – and a dominant one. It must not regard its rider as a parasite which must be got rid of at any cost, nor as an almost unendurable burden which handicaps its style and ability.

It is always difficult for the human brain to understand precisely what goes on in the mind of a colt or filly when first asked to carry a human being on its back; something not included in the inherited list of stimuli and natural responses. It needs a special kind of mentality to make the acceptance of such an imposition feasible.

In human relationships the enforcement of a burden of this kind would be intolerable. A mother will carry her baby and devote her whole attention to so doing, but it is the mother, the carrier, who remains the dominant party.

In the mental make-up of the horse there must be some special quality of submission we do not fully understand.

A camel may become a beast of burden. To an elephant the conveyance of a hundredweight of human flesh means very little, and having accepted a man as its master on the ground it is no great hardship to carry him on its back. But no other animal would be prepared to enter into a similar relationship with man even if it possessed the strength to do so. The ass and the mule accepted the burden under compulsion, but not the zebra which flatly refused to be coerced into submission or into any voluntary association with mankind. Few members of the ruminants, either ox or deer, would permit themselves to sink to such depths of degradation as to carry a man on their backs.

Even in the case of the horse, this sudden disturbance introduced into its life at only 2 years of age may be an experience from which the equine temperament never really recovers. In some individuals it leaves a mental scar apt to set up irritation on occasion, even long after the burden has been accepted or tolerated. It may give rise to the 'rogue' or in milder cases to the horse that may 'play up' under very little extra provocation.

Horses and dogs exhibited several marked differences prior to domestication. The dog could be persuaded to join the family circle, being attracted by human company and by the food and shelter which went with it. It enjoyed being accepted and exhibited signs of understanding the relationship between reward and performance. If a dog carried out some kind of action and was rewarded on each occasion by a gift of food or even by a kind word, it regarded the reward as recompense for satisfactory behaviour and was willing to repeat the behaviour for further reward.

During training, the horse is often more ready than the dog to carry out some kind of 'work' without reward, whenever the task it is called upon to execute is in no way contrary to whatever it likes doing.

Occasionally, however, the horse might be coerced by patient training into doing something against its own wishes. If the training was continued at reasonable intervals the horse became accustomed to performing in some particular manner. In other words, it developed a habit, not very dissimilar to the type of conditioned reflex Pavlov introduced into his dogs. This kind of education is utilised today in dressage training and in persuading horses to repeat at frequent intervals the tricks and antics which delight circus audiences. We will discuss this phase of tuition at greater length in a later chapter.

I mention these psychological details only to point out some of the reasons why the horse, out of all the assorted animals living in the swamps and later on the plains, became amenable to entering into companionship and co-operation with an animal so basically different in every way as man.

No greater contrast can be imagined than that existing between the four-legged horse and the two-legged man with his upright stance, with arms and a pair of hands in place of forelimbs with hoofs attached.

The attraction, if attraction there was, must have lain in man's higher mental development which enabled him to think for the horse as well as for himself, and to develop a system of messages understood by the animal. This could never have been achieved had not the horse that peculiar perceptiveness, the kind of mentality and temperament, which made it possible for it to receive and translate these messages from the human brain, whether they were transmitted by touch or by the voice.

Many have ascribed to the horse the possession of a sixth sense, a form of telepathy, by means of which the horse knows what is going on in the mind of its master or its rider (see Chapter 9). It appears more likely, however, that such messages are received through the medium of touch and to a lesser degree sound, rather than through any additional channel. Telepathy may, of course, be one of the senses we ourselves have lost during the process of evolution and it could be that certain animals still retain it. But, failing this, it would imply the possession of a type of mind not likely to be found within the usual domestic circle of man and his animals.

It is possible, however, that in some species other than horses a similar responsiveness to the human will might be encouraged if only one could overcome their natural fear of mankind. This is difficult to achieve, although the horse can be conditioned to human presence and touch in a very short time, so long as the human being carrying out the conditioning is also possessed of that rather special type of mentality, which makes him or her acceptable to the subject being so influenced.

The North American Indian when, as usually happened, he was also a horseman, could select a horse from a flock of completely wild creatures, rope it, approach and handle it, place a loop of rope in its mouth and a blanket on its back, mount and ride it out on to the prairie under a reasonable degree of control within forty-eight hours of first setting eyes upon it.

All of which goes to show that the Indian knew how to instil confidence, banish fear and convey a series of messages to the horse's mind. It showed, equally convincingly, that the horse possessed the type of mentality capable of understanding, and trusting the Indian, without fear of the man or his intentions. It is likely that such a horse not only tolerated but actually enjoyed contact, mental and physical, with the man, and that it was willing to learn to carry out any reasonable pattern of behaviour which the man suggested and the horse understood.

Probably the horse discovered sooner or later that this sort of partnership guaranteed it food, and protection against marauding animals, and although the horse may not have been capable of estimating the advantages and disadvantages of such a situation, it is likely that it realised that its present existence compared favourably with its past, and like all animals lower than man, being less concerned with the future than with the present, it was quite willing to continue in a partnership which was proving to be such an agreeable one.

It must have required a considerable degree of trust in his own relationship with a wild animal and his ability to convey messages from his own mind to that of the horse in question – not to mention courage – before the Indian could make up his mind to mount the horse, sit astride its back, and with only a leather thong attached to its lower jaw, with the other end held in his hand, permit it to set off with him at full gallop across the prairie secure in the belief that he would be able to stop it when required, steer it and persuade it to return with him, still mounted upon it, to his human habitation.

That such ability is not confined to the North American Indian is shown by a paragraph contributed to *Horse and Hound* in 1963 by 'Observer'. He recalls how Dr Hector Geddes, senior lecturer in animal husbandry at the University of Sydney, New South Wales, demonstrated in this country a method of breaking wild horses that had been taught him by an old Australian horseman, Mr K. Jefferies, who could catch, gentle and back a wild horse in an hour. After showing a film of Mr Jefferies in action, Dr Geddes gave a personal demonstration using a two-year-old colt that had never been caught. Dr Geddes caught, gentled, bridled and mounted the pony within three minutes of the allotted hour. He then removed the bridle and remounted the pony to show how quiet it was after handling.

This book is concerned with the equine mind rather than the human, but the fact that, in addition to the North American Indian riders, both Mr Jefferies and Dr Geddes were able to accomplish this feat, provides ample evidence that the right kind of human mind can gain ascendancy or exhibit some hypnotic influence over at least a proportion of the equine specimens with which it comes into contact.

Although such ability can be exercised by most people who are in sympathetic touch with a dog, it is certain that even an Indian, accustomed to horses from birth, would not have succeeded in similar fashion with many varieties other than the horse. The feat would have proved impossible with a giraffe, supposing such an animal had been available, nor would it have been feasible with a buffalo, a bison or with any other wild ruminant. These animals lack the mental mechanism which makes it possible for them to enter into any sort of voluntary partnership with man.

When visiting a zoological garden, especially a walled one as opposed to those which permit freedom of range, one is apt to wonder whether animals are happier living a wild life, frequently struggling for an existence, assailed by various marauding animals equally hungry for their flesh, or when warmly ensconced in a cage with plenty of bedding, regular meals served by a human being, with complete freedom from any danger other than fire and disease.

Do animals in their cages regard these as their natural habitat and home, and the world outside merely as a larger cage peopled by unfortunates compelled to fend for themselves without the security and protection they themselves enjoy?

People who rear young wild birds in outdoor aviaries have extreme difficulty in persuading them to enter the outside world even when the aviary doors are left wide open.

Horses living in droves in a swamp or on the plains permitted their lives to be directed by a series of instinctive responses to well-recognised stimuli without the exercise of conscious thought. Seeing that these same responses had carried many generations of horses through life without a hitch, it would seem that there was no call for thought. Such horses had little need to think or reason, even if they had possessed the mental equipment for the purpose.

All horses needed to do, except fill their stomachs, was to keep in close formation, and remain as near the centre of the group as possible since the stragglers on the outskirts were the first to succumb to marauding carnivores. The younger stallions were compelled by the older dominant sires to keep on the fringe of the drove, well away from the mares, which being all-important from the standpoint of survival were lodged in the centre. Although it was undoubtedly the intention of the dominant stallion to insist upon this rigid segregation of the sexes, it is not at all certain that it always materialised. Ruling stallions must nod sometimes and feminine curiosity is strong even in equine circles. It is likely that they, too, sometimes took advantage of the siesta enjoyed by their lord and master to find out what went on at the outer fringe of their encirclement.

These young males had no great value within their own community other than as sentries, especially in the opinion of the ruling stallion. Being no braver than sentries of other species, they advertised their own presence, as well as the propinquity of enemies, by one shrill neigh emitted whenever their courage reached a low ebb. This would be the signal for the whole drove to vanish, galloping away across the plain for perhaps a quarter of a mile before coming to a halt.

The sentry uttering the warning signal might succeed in rejoining his company, but it is more likely that any marauder would position itself in such a way as to cut off the retreat of the unfortunate animal.

It would be a mistake to imagine that primitive horses living in their natural surroundings were in the habit of galloping long distances on the flat, uphill or down dale. Their terrain was in all probability flat and marshy and not conducive to anything more than short sprints. In all probability few would ever gallop more than a quarter of a mile and then only in company, and it is even likely that galloping blindly at speed into fresh country might land the horses amid greater danger than that from which they were retreating.

The animals which preyed upon the horses were often very fast over a matter of a hundred yards or more, but were unable to maintain the pace over longer distances. Like the horses they were in no sense of the word 'stayers' capable of following their prey for great distances. Possibly the wolves were the only animals at that time capable of keeping up a prolonged chase and wolves were to be found in most parts of the world during the times when horses roamed the marshes on multi-toed feet.

But a large drove of horses, especially when headed by one or two vicious stallions, would congregate into close formation and armed with hoofs and teeth were no easy prey for a few wolves. No doubt the wolves soon became aware of the fact and attacked only in large packs. The circle of horses, crowded together with heads in the centre and feet lashing out furiously at the periphery, were capable of keeping a good many wolves at a respectful distance. If the horses broke formation and started to gallop it is likely that only those with considerable staying power could avoid capture and these possibly survived to propagate their species.

The wild horse undoubtedly became very expert at getting away at a fast pace from possible enemies, even if on many occasions one of the young stallions called 'Wolf', when there was little occasion so to do.

But it must never be imagined that primitive horses would ever have galloped two and a half to four miles over jumping country as so many steeplechasers are expected to do nowadays, although there is not the least doubt that the ancient horse was fleet of foot over a short distance.

This escape reflex, the response to alarm or even to a mild suspicion of danger, was and remains inherent in the species, and it was further conditioned by experience and circumstance. Those horses which tarried were soon eliminated, even if the tarrying resulted only in the individual being left behind and dependent upon its own resources, this being a state of affairs with which few horses can cope. Only the fastest and the fittest remained to reproduce their kind and so the tendency was to establish a faster animal and one quickly off the mark in face of doubt or danger.

The runaway horse of today is only carrying out the kind of behaviour which made it possible for its ancestors to survive, even if today there are no four-legged wolves at large in this country.

The horse at pasture has an excellent ability to recognise the approach of strange people or strange animals for, as we will read in the chapter dealing with equine vision, it is able to see straight ahead, or on both sides of the body at the same time, one eye taking in the right side and the other the left.

Moreover, the horse, standing squarely, sees a good deal of what goes on behind its body without turning its head. This is modified to some extent according to the width of the shoulders and buttocks.

When grazing and actually picking grass with mouth to ground, the horse can see everything that goes on all around its body (within a limited horizon) even at the rear end, simply by gazing between its own legs and feet (See Fig. 5.)

Fig. 5. When grazing, a horse, by looking between its limbs, can see in every direction – front, sides and behind – and is immediately aware of the approach of another animal. The ears pick up sounds, and earth vibrations are felt through the teeth, jaws, bones of the head and the limbs.

When the horse forsook the marshes and sought the higher ground, the plains and the hills, life began to take on a different aspect. Not only was the ground underfoot drier and much firmer, it was in places extremely hard and also rough and rocky. By this time it is to be presumed that the horse had developed the single toe and the new terrain must have proved a sore trial.

It was clear now that a satisfactory survival ratio ran parallel with the possession of well-shaped feet with good sound heels, good bars and wide deep frogs. The latter, in company with the bars, acted as buffers which minimised the damage which concussion did to the limbs and body. The frog and bars of the new type of foot also acted as a non-skid device and helped considerably in the process of coming to a halt from a rapid pace.

Today it is said that a horse is only as good as its feet – or as some experienced horsemen now put it, 'as its farrier'.

But on good grazing ground unshod feet were quite satisfactory provided they were of sound construction and it was mainly on account of the wear occasioned to their feet that horses were compelled to remain within reasonable distance of their water supply in districts where that commodity was not too plentiful. The horse being originally devised as a creature of the swamps still needs a good deal of water.

Had horses roamed far into the rocky heights their feet would have suffered. The walls would have broken away and laminitis would have supervened. Most of our modern indigenous ponies have rather upright walls, a box-like foot, with high heels, good bars and frogs. It is these animals which provide the best pointer to the kind of foot possessed by horses before the days of domestication.

It is even possible that the development of the soliped condition in place of the original multi-toed foot, by limiting the range of the horse's movements and encouraging the herding of horses into limited areas, or in parts of the country well supplied with water, has been one of the main reasons why the species has maintained its existence through so many thousands of years.

2

The Influence of Domestication

The metamorphosis which has taken place in the horse during thousands of centuries has necessarily accompanied a complete change in environment, and pattern of living. This has resulted in the development of a new type of behaviour and special adaptation to circumstance. One might argue that it has created a need for a degree of intelligence greatly superior to that existing in the primitive ancestor. In this one might quite well be wrong. One must make a distinction between intelligence untutored and the same degree of intelligence awakened by education.

There is no reason to suppose that the brain of the horse today is in any way dissimilar from that of the horse of five thousand years ago. It is true that brain weight increased or diminished according to the size of the horse or pony, but there is no evidence to prove that a large horse with a correspondingly larger brain is any more intelligent than the pony with a small brain. Often the converse is far nearer the truth.

The brain of man has altered through the ages because it has developed more convolutions and these carry a far more extensive measure of grey matter.

Beneath all this additional grey matter the primitive brain still lies, whether the subject be man or horse, and in times of stress or great excitement the primitive brain, as I have said, is apt to assume control.

There is little reason to believe that the brain of the chimpanzee of today is any more highly developed than it was thousands of years ago, but chimpanzees sometimes live now in close companionship with human beings, behave themselves, more or less, at informal tea parties, wear clothes and smoke cigarettes, simply as the result of tuition, an education of the mind, denied the chimpanzee in earlier times.

Very much the same thing has happened to the horse. It has been educated and taught to respond to stimuli quite different from those which controlled its behaviour in the days of long ago. All it then had to do was to keep an eye upon the dominant stallion, the leader of the herd, or maybe occasionally upon a progressive type of female who quite possibly during the cold weather, when breeding operations were dormant, took over the leadership. Other horses simply followed their behaviour.

When the 'boss' stood still and listened, the others did likewise. When the 'boss' decided it was an appropriate moment to make a rapid getaway, or even to make a leisurely move into some other neighbourhood, the others all followed without question. When the 'boss' called a halt, all came to a standstill together.

This series of actions covered everything necessary in an equine Elysium, where all one had to do was eat, sleep, produce foals and keep away from dangerous animals.

At the present time it has to contend with no dangerous animals other than man. From its own adopted 'boss', the horse now receives regular meals, accommodation indoors or out of doors, and needs exert itself only when its 'boss' arrives in breeches or jodhpurs and demands its attention and co-operation.

It does not take a horse long to learn to pass through a doorway into a loose box in which it will find a manger containing oats and bran, nor to carry a living weight upon its back.

It learns that a pull on the bit, accompanied by the spoken sound 'Whoa!', means that it must come to a standstill. Before long it may become conditioned to doing this when it hears the sound without any corresponding tug on the bit or reins, or it may answer to the tug without the 'Whoa!'

It learns also that an unspellable sound created by man when he produces a vacuum between the tip of his tongue and the roof of his mouth, must act as the stimulus which advises it to put on speed, even when it is already going at its fastest. It is likely that at an early stage of its tuition the horse learned that the unpronounceable sound was usually accompanied by a light cut with the whip and accordingly it became accustomed to producing the right response, quite consciously in order to avoid the pain of the lash.

The main difference between the mentality of the modern horse and that of the wild horse prior to domestication lies in the degree of ability it shows in establishing mental contact with its owner, attendant or rider, and in making adequate response to stimuli quite unknown to its primitive ancestors.

Such stimuli induce modern horses to walk, trot and canter in preordained patterns unlike their natural gaits; jump over a variety of seemingly impossible obstacles, then come again to a standstill at the rider's will. These stimuli may be transmitted to the horse merely by differences in the pressure exerted upon the animal's body by the rider's limbs.

Such messages may also be conveyed to the horse's mind via its mouth through the reins and bit, or to its ears by sounds issuing from the human mouth.

It must not be presumed that every primitive horse could, had the opportunity arisen, have been trained to do all these things at the wish of the rider, had one existed. Nor must it be imagined that every modern descendant of the primitive horse can be persuaded to do them either. Whether a rank refusal to accept man as the leader, and a strong objection to becoming his plaything, denotes a higher degree of intelligence, a spirit of independence, or is to be accepted as an indication of mental retardation, is still a question concerning which one may experience a reasonable doubt.

It is possible that in the days that preceded domestication these rebels also appeared, horses unwilling to accept leadership and determined to go their own way through life. Whether such pretensions were practicable or if the solitary horse was at the mercy of beasts of prey cannot now be decided.

One cannot psycho-analyse a horse and perhaps nothing is lost on this account. What has happened during the last few hundred years at least is that bad-tempered stallions have been gelded, unless they happened to be particularly fast, or excellent stayers upon the race track; and mares displaying a vicious spirit or too much independence have seldom been bred from. As a result, only those horses which have shown a suitable respect for the wishes of mankind have had opportunity to produce any progeny and these would in all likelihood be free from such undesirable characteristics. Occasionally, however, the rogue still turns up and we will write more concerning this type of animal later.

There are still breeds of horses in existence which neither desire to enjoy the society of mankind nor pander to human wishes. Such animals never willingly establish mental contact with other than their own kind.

The broncho, a member of a half-tamed type rather than a breed, is an example, but it must be remembered that a particular kind of behaviour is encouraged in this type of horse by ill-treatment, tight girthing and other measures which antagonise the animal from the time it first sets eyes on man, its tormentor. As a result, the broncho will do everything possible to throw its human rider sky-high and refuses to submit to the indignity of carrying a man upon its back.

These 'mean' horses, as the ranchers term them, are usually normal in all other respects apart from their hatred of man, and if one views their attitude objectively, one may come to the conclusion that their behaviour does not necessarily imply the possession of a low order of intelligence – in fact it is almost typical of the way in which any full-blooded human being would behave in similar circumstances.

The obligation imposed upon the horse, that it should, at any selected moment, conform to the will of its owner by galloping an excessive distance at high speed and jumping a number of difficult obstacles on the way, gave rise to another equine need. It made it essential that the modern hurdler, steeplechaser or show jumper should be provided with a bigger chest cavity, more capacious lungs and a type of heart, superior to those with which primitive horses were endowed.

It necessitated, also, various other changes in the conformation of body and limbs in order to qualify the horse for the performance of tasks of a kind for which it was never created. In addition, the horse was expected to endure during long, hard-ridden races, a maximum of fatigue calculated to bring it to the very limit of its physical resources, to make no mention of the degree of mental agony involved in such an experience.

To produce horses willing and capable of enduring such a degree of self-sacrifice took centuries of selective breeding, eliminating strains which did not prove equal to the task and retaining certain bloodlines which showed promise of success. It must be remembered, though, that the improvement in type was not brought about wholly with the object of producing a better horse, but one calculated to win more money.

It must not be imagined that such feats of endurance and speed are performed entirely out of the horse's own volition. The horse is a very sensitive animal, easily stirred into activity by a degree of excitement aroused within it in sympathy with that experienced by its rider, suggested and transmitted to it by tactile sensations passing between rider and horse.

It must be remembered that the horse in its normal environment galloped only when fear or panic gave rise within its mind to a realisation of the need to escape. The danger lying behind this need was apparent to the leader and by a system akin to telepathy, or possibly by some other expression, a sense of panic was conveyed by the leader to the members of the herd. All then experienced the same response to fear and galloped away at their fastest pace for as far as the leader considered essential to safety.

But, if by any chance the danger continued to pursue, then the leader would urge on its followers to maintain the pace to the point of near-exhaustion. This is precisely what happens in a race, the part of the leader being played by the human jockey, who, by suggestion conveyed to the horse, persuades it that the need to gallop at its hardest is imperative for its safety. When a number of horses are engaged in a race they revert to the type of behaviour which prevailed in the days when horses lived in herds or droves, ready to make a rapid getaway but inclined to slow down when they think themselves safe to do so.

Whether a horse happened to be a little behind or in front of another was not so important, provided it was establishing distance between itself and a potential or imaginary enemy; in

35

fact to be in the middle of a group was the safest position so long as the whole group maintained the necessary speed.

Today, it is all-important that a horse shall at a certain point in the gallop – i.e. at the 'winning post' – be *in front* of all the other horses if it is at all possible.

Only the jockeys know where this so-called winning post lies and none of the horses has any knowledge of its whereabouts or even of its existence. It follows therefore that the struggle to arrive at this point ahead of all the other horses and riders exists only in the minds of the jockeys. It is their ability to arouse their mounts to produce more and more speed which decides which will be the winner and which the 'also-rans'.

Success need not depend so much upon the ability of the horse to produce the greatest speed – to travel a certain distance in the least time – as upon the ability of the jockey to excite his mount to the necessary degree of enthusiasm, panic, or whatever emotion induces it to put forth its full amount of energy. He must do this at a critical moment during the race.

The truth is that, if races could be run more than once under exactly the same circumstances, the results would seldom tally. On some days horses of equal fitness will put up a better jockey-response than on others; and although trainers estimate the ability of their horses on the principle that so many additional ounces carried on the horse's back is equivalent to so many more or less paces, or even so many feet or yards in each mile, they are presuming that each horse in the race is consistently producing the best speed of which it is capable, and they are making no allowances for the degree of response which can be elicited from any particular horse on any particular day by any particular jockey.

There are a great many reasons other than induced response which may produce a deal of variation in a horse's speed over any given distance and these will be considered again later.

But the horse in many ways resembles other domesticated animals – the dog and the cat as well as man himself – in being unable totally to discard all primitive responses in favour of those instilled into it as the result of education. No enforcement of discipline can prevent any one of this group of animals becoming completely out of control and behaving in truly primitive animal fashion when sudden danger threatens, or appears to the animal to do so. Disturbed by fear, the horse will forget all about its submission to human control. It will take hold of the bit, turn tail and gallop, often into greater danger than any it could be leaving behind, because it now lives not in a swamp but in a world of highways and of fast-moving traffic among which stampede brings disaster.

Horses appear to be imaginative creatures capable of seeing visions, although this may possibly be due to the fact that their eyes are often at fault in a world of rapid movement and are incapable of rapid changes of focus. The subject of equine vision will be dealt with more fully in Chapter 4.

Since horses have considerable difficulty in focusing two eyes simultaneously upon an object a little way ahead, they are apt to mistake some harmless object such as a stone standing out prominently from a hedge, a patch of sand, or some chaff or straw spilt upon an otherwise clean country road, as something possibly fraught with danger. When such a sight conjures up an instinctive memory of dreadful things that happened to horses countless years ago, the horse may suddenly obey the stimulus that a similar sight might have produced in its ancestors. It may then respond by 'shying', jumping over the object or bolting, or by exhibiting some peculiar pattern of behaviour very unpleasant in the opinion of its novice rider.

A great many years ago near Falmouth in the county of Cornwall there existed one place on a main country thoroughfare where practically every horse passing a certain corner of the road would sweat and tremble, shy away from it furiously and endeavour to bolt. The place received the name 'Hard-to-come-by', which, phonetically abbreviated, still figures in the Ordnance maps. So frequently did accidents arise at this spot that the particular hedge had to be demolished and rebuilt in different form. Nothing to account for the alarm it produced in horses was discovered and it seems obvious that the horses themselves did not fully understand the reason for their panic. The stimulus producing this response was probably inherited and based upon some past memory. I deal with this subject more fully in Chapter 9.

An object, at one time very familiar in country districts, was the steam engine which pulled large trucks loaded with stones along the highways on massive iron wheels. Another similar sight was the steam-roller which rolled the same stones into the road surface. It is quite certain that every horse and pony regarded these large vehicles with their high chimneys as some kind of prehistoric animal puffing flame and steam out of a solitary nostril. In any case, whenever one of these alarming pieces of mechanism was operating within a distance of one mile, every hunter resting in its stable, every horse pulling a gig or carrying a rider on its back, would sweat, snort, stamp, and, if on the road, would refuse to move another inch in its direction. Usually it took the combined efforts of the driver or rider, now dismounted, together with those of the man carrying the red flag in front of the engine, to persuade the horse to pass the steaming monster.

It mattered not in the least how many times the horse encountered the same engine, the result was always the same; it never became accustomed to or lost its fear of the steam engine. Fortunately, in those days horse traffic on country roads, apart from the main thoroughfares, was very sparse, otherwise the engine driver and his flagman would have rolled in very few stones.

There is little doubt that such manifestations of panic which induced so many horses to ignore all the teaching they had received, to lose confidence in their new 'bosses' and to take no notice of the instructions issued to them, stirred up impressions left in the primitive brain. These were possibly associated with the days when it was not unusual to observe flames and steam issuing from volcanic eruptions. This may appear a little far-fetched as a theory but no better one presents itself.

Even now, many years later, very few horses can be trusted on roads where mechanical vehicles are in rapid movement, in spite of the fact that these are very silent when compared with the 'Puffing Billies' of half a century ago.

All of which goes to show that when the horse exchanged the marshes for the plains, and the plains for a life of domestication under man's leadership, it changed also its mode of life and its normal pattern of behaviour for another, which, on all but a few occasions, rendered it necessary for the horse to 'forget', or replace the old responses by entirely new ones.

Now that the craze for speed has developed a race of mechanically minded human beings, the horse can retain a place in the world by virtue only of its remarkable powers of adaptation. By the exercise of these powers it has gained a new position in the life of the people as a companion in sports and games (though still remaining a servant) and also acts as an auxiliary nursemaid or nannie in numerous homes which possess children and sufficient wealth to supply them with ponies.

If, in a great many cases, the existence of the horse depends mainly upon its ability to provide all classes of people with the excitement of a financial flutter, we must accept the fact with gratitude, so long as such ability provides the excuse and ensures the continued presence of the horse in our midst.

3

Horse Senses

An animal as alert as the horse and responsive to such a variety of stimuli must of necessity be provided with a very active nervous mechanism.

Horses, however, like people, differ very considerably in temperament. A few – very few one might say – are sluggish, but these may represent retarded specimens below average mentality, such as may occur in any species of animal. Far more horses are inclined to become over-excited with very little stimulation. As has already been explained, the right kind of nervous system needs to be partnered by a conformation and physique capable of withstanding intense, prolonged exertion, all of which necessitates the presence of equally good circulatory and respiratory systems.

To sum this up, the horse, whether it be a racehorse, hunter, show jumper or even a pony owned by the modern child rider, needs to be bodily sound, intelligent and provided with an efficient heart and lungs. It must be temperamentally stable and able to profit by education.

One might include the hope that such a paragon in the physical and mental respects might also be a model for the artist, an example of perfect conformation. Strange as it may seem, beauty of form and performance in the field do not always run in double harness.

Horses of all shapes and sizes, good-looking horses, ugly horses and downright cripples, sometimes win races. Races of great value often fall to classically bred horses of nondescript appearance, while the artist's models trail along in the rear.

It is true that the winning of classic races by horses of dubious value from the standpoint of conformation may be the exception rather than the rule but the exception occasionally crops up, frequently enough to suggest that stamina is something inherent in certain horses, often associated more with the mental capacity to endure over-exertion than with bodily perfection.

The history of humanity teems with similar stories of great endeavour carried out by persons who seemed least qualified physically to perform such feats of endurance and courage.

To most discerning people the English Thoroughbred is easily the most beautiful of all creatures bred by man. Although it carries a great deal of Eastern blood, the introduction was fortunately fruitful. I use the word 'fortunately' because no Eastern horse, whether Arabian, Barbary or Tartary in origin, could today compete in a race for speed with any good Thoroughbred. It so happened that the Eastern blood 'nicked', as breeders say, with that of the English mares at the end of the 17th century and thereby produced progeny superior to their sires and dams. These colts and fillies, mated together with considerable care in their selection, produced our modern racehorse, which combined the endurance and stamina of the Eastern horse with the activity and better conformation of the English mares.

The improvement in the racehorse has been steadily maintained by selective breeding during the past 250 years. Had a similar interest not been taken in our own home-bred stock between the reigns of Richard I and Charles II there would have been no mares in this country likely to profit by the fortuitous introduction of Eastern blood. The latter sires certainly improved stamina and lent distance and endurance to the resulting progeny, but speed derives from the old British stock and today's sprinters probably owe very little to their alien blood.

It must not be inferred, from anything written so far in this book, that good conformation is not a highly desirable feature. It is something to be aimed at, particularly if one maintains a stud, partially at least, by the sale of foals. All that has been implied is that many horses win races not on account of their beauty, but because they are mentally equipped with a willingness to sacrifice themselves, even their lives, for a little extra speed or another furlong beyond their normal capacity.

One cannot fail to be impressed by the inherent vitality of the horse, especially the English Throughbred. Intensely alert and responsive to every sound and movement, it becomes apparent to the least experienced observer that, even if the horse does little to analyse the sights and sounds in its vicinity, it is extremely responsive to them immediately upon their reception, even before there has been time to decide whether they carry any dangerous portent or not. It is this quick responsiveness which keeps the horse always in a state of high tension, ever ready to put a large amount of space between itself and danger with the least possible delay.

In people and horses alike, pluck and will power provide the fuel which propels the body to perform great deeds. In horses, at least, these attributes are often found in certain bloodlines.

Although it is a joy when one finds perfection of form in company with a brilliant performance and an exhibition of great stamina, it must also be remembered that these two virtues are not inseparable.

Stamina is a difficult word to define. It can only exist when lungs and heart muscle are basically sound, and its presence seems to depend upon true synchronisation between the mental and physical apparatus rather than upon external bodily shape. In some instances bodily handicaps can be compensated for by superior courage and a deal of determination.

Stamina implies or denotes endurance, but in the Thoroughbred horse it includes something more – the ability to force the body to achieve a miracle in an emergency.

Our indigenous ponies *are* and, until they virtually disappeared, our carthorses *were* possessed of great endurance in the work they were called upon to perform, but the Thoroughbred horse and some of its close relations, carrying a little of the blood of its three famous ancestors, are able to produce on occasion that little extra spurt of speed, the ability to gallop a little faster and a little further, by virtue of the influence of brain upon body.

How great a part the jockey plays in stimulating the horse to greater feats has already been discussed and undoubtedly it is considerable.

But races are not won with the whip. Many horses go on strike when they are cruelly treated and a whipped horse is usually already a beaten one. That little bit extra which wins the race is more frequently due to a transfusion of enthusiasm from the brain of the rider into that of the horse.

What kind of a brain does the horse possess?

Compared with the size of the horse's head the brain appears rather small; but the head must be large because it contains voluminous air sinuses as well as lengthy nasal passages, leaving a comparatively small space to form the cranial cavity in which the brain is lodged.

The brain itself is quite well-developed with a considerable number of convolutions and a fair thickness of grey matter covering them. Of course, it does not compare in any way with that of any of the Primates. But it has a very good pattern of communications both between different nerve centres and between the brain, the body and limbs. The brain of the horse was specially suitable to the requirements of an animal living by grazing and constantly on the lookout for those marauding animals which had a special liking for horseflesh. That of the English Thoroughbred has been improved by selection and those horses which were unwilling to sacrifice their bodies in order to set up a record, either for speed or endurance, have been culled. Since keeping unprofitable racehorses costs money, this has been done for no altruistic reason but on grounds of sheer economy.

The result has been the improvement of the Thoroughbred and the production of animals capable of great speed over a comparatively short distance; and of others capable of travelling up to two and a half or even four miles over jumps. Naturally the last type of race is run more slowly than a similar distance on the flat, but the energy expended is greater. The modern horse, racing over jumps of any kind, has to go the whole distance without serious mistake, and without slackening speed a fraction during the whole distance.

It is unfortunate in many respects that Thoroughbreds of only two years, unformed, only partly grown and comparatively green, should be required to race over distances of five furlongs before the Derby meeting and six furlongs after September 1st. There is no doubt that many promising youngsters are ruined in this way or at least seriously handicapped in later life. These races for two-year-olds are held during the spring at all the principal meetings and most of those engaged will have run at least once before the Ascot Meeting held in June.

While racing can only be practised by a great many owners in this way, hoping to win sufficient in stake money with a two-year-old to keep it during the next two years, these Thoroughbred infants will continue to be raced.

The brain centres dealing with vision and hearing in the horse are highly efficient in keeping with the horse's needs. One sense which the horse shares with most of the other hoofed animals, whether they possess the single toe or the cloven hoof, and also with many animals which move about on foot pads, is the ability to appreciate ground vibrations so slight that we ourselves have no practical acquaintance with them.

The tremors created on the surface of the earth by the feet of other animals, even when some distance away, are transmitted through the ground and to the limb bones of those animals able to detect them. Not only are such vibrations picked up by solid horny hoofs, but they are also perceived through the foot pads and possibly through the nails of a great many of the soft-footed species, including such animals as the dog, fox, rabbit and hare.

Although vibrations at the earth's surface may not be so evident on soft ground as on hard, they are, nevertheless, transmitted through the limb bones, carried to the skull and registered by the internal and middle ear. It is even possible that the large air cavities in the skull act as sound boxes and amplify the ground vibrations.

A horse grazing in a field can detect the footsteps of a man or of another horse on the hard road long before they become actually audible and often a considerable time before the owner of the feet hoves into view. This is particularly easy for horses standing still on all four feet as the front limb bones, the radius and ulna, the knee bones, canons and pasterns are locked, and the passage of vibrations up and through them is facilitated.

Our own feet and limbs have lost this ability, if they ever possessed it, probably because we insulate our soles with footwear, but many of the African tribes who travel barefooted retain it to a remarkable degree.

4

Vision in the Horse

The horse exhibits one marked peculiarity, which in lesser degree is shown by some of the two-clawed ungulates. It is the method by which it focuses its eyes on to both near and distant objects.

The majority of animals, from man down to fishes and reptiles, focus their vision by altering the shape of the lens, or by moving the lens nearer or further from the cornea, the transparent window in front of the eye. This causes the rays of light which pass through the lens at an angle with each other to meet upon the retina, which is the receiving membrane lining the hinder part of the eyeball, in such a way that they convey impressions along the optic nerve and produce a clear image at the visual centre in the hinder part of the brain.

In these animals the retina is regularly concave. In the horse the retina is *irregularly* concave, being nearer the cornea at some parts than at others, giving rise to what is known as a 'ramped retina'.

In the horse the ciliary muscle which operates the shape of the lens in most other animals is poorly developed, and the horse depends upon this ramped retina for its ability to focus its eyes.

The retina, although an elaborate structure comprising a number of layers of nerve cells and nerve connections, appears as a thin transparent membrane lining the hinder part of the eyeball and resting upon the choroid coat which is black. Such pigmentation of the choroid ensures that the light rays are not wasted through absorption and enables them to exert their full force upon the highly sensitive retina.

This applies equally to the eyes of most animals, but the horse is different in a rather peculiar way. It makes use of the irregularity in the degree of concavity in different parts of the retina and it contrives by lifting or lowering the head to enable the rays of light to meet upon the particular part of the cornea which will produce the best visual image.

As a result of the manner in which the concavity of the retina varies, the distance from the centre of the lens to the centre of the retina will be slightly less than that from the centre of the lens to any part of the retina lying below its centre (see Fig. 6).

In actual measurements, taking the eye of the Thoroughbred horse as a pattern, the distance from the cornea to the upper part of the retina will be 45 mm.; from the cornea to the central part of the retina it will be 43 mm.; and from the cornea to the lowest part of the retina it will be 40 mm.

In the lower part of the retina lies the optic disc, the point at which the optic nerve enters and spreads out within the retina. This is the so-called 'blind spot', found also in our own eyes.

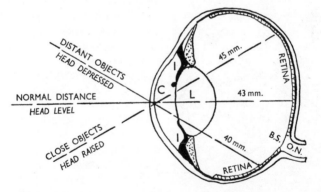

Fig. 6. Section of the eye of the horse. This shows how the horse contrives to focus upon objects by simply raising or lowering its head so that the rays of light fall upon a different part of the retina. This is due to the retina being 'ramped', in that it does not form a true arc of a circle and provides a different focal length according to each change in the position of the head. This cannot occur if the horse is ridden with a tight rein – and especially with a martingale. C. Cornea; L. Lens; O.N. Optic nerve; B.S. the 'blind spot' where the optic nerve enters the retina.

It follows, therefore, that the ability of the horse to focus to enable it to see an object clearly depends upon its ability to move its head freely. By raising or lowering it or by tilting it a little sideways, the horse obtains the optimum focus and the clearest possible image. (Fig. 7.)

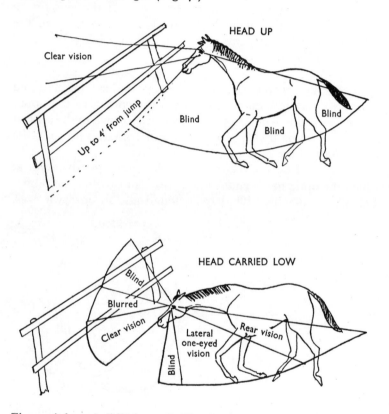

Fig. 7. A horse's 'blind spots'. The drawings show how the rays of light may fall upon two eyes directed forwards, in the one case with the head carried high and in the other with it carried low. It is likely that the horse sees two pictures, except when both eyes are converged forwards, as when taking stock of a jump. The two pictures may be viewed simultaneously, one with either eye, on the corresponding side of the body. The horse will also have a fairly clear view of what goes on behind its body, but when looking straight ahead can see nothing on either side.

1. The take-off for a jump: Lt.-Colonel J. A. Talbot-Ponsonby schooling a horse at his Instructional Riding Centre at Todenham, Gloucestershire.

2. The airborne period: Captain Raimondo d'Inzeo on 'The Quiet Man'. (See pp. 59–61.)

3. The landing: Lt.-Colonel Talbot-Ponsonby at the end of a jump. (See p. 60.)

4. 'Most of us have at some time or other watched trick horses in circuses.' Twelve young Friesian stallions trained by Mr Rudolf Jurkschat. (See p. 93.)

If the head be raised high the light rays fall upon the lower part of the retina; if it be held low with the eyes directed downward, the rays will fall upon the upper part. In the former case the focal length will be 40 mm. and in the latter 45 mm. The closer the object viewed the greater is the focal length from cornea to retina.

Incidentally, almost every horse suffers more or less from astigmatism as neither its cornea nor its lens is truly shaped. To give some idea of what this implies, a person suffering from astigmatism, when looking at the face of a clock for instance, does not see all its figures equally well. The IX or the X may appear sharper than certain other figures on the dial such as the III or the V.

We are able to correct our visual errors with the aid of glasses in which the lenses are cut in such a way as to restore our vision to normal. The horse cannot make use of such aids.

In order to establish a correct focus and a clear, well-defined image, the diverging rays of light passing through the cornea and lens must *meet* upon the correct part of the sensitive retinal surface. If they meet a little in front of or behind it the image will be more or less blurred.

In order that the rays shall actually meet on the horse's retina it is essential that the head and the eye shall be in the right position so that the horse may instinctively direct the light rays on to the exact spot of the peculiar ramped retina.

Fig. 6 will show what this implies.

The eyes of the horse are not placed truly frontally as in man, monkeys and some of the short-faced breeds of dogs, but are arranged somewhat obliquely or laterally, as they are in most varieties of animals which were hunted when they lived in a wild state. Not, of course, in the sense that we hunt our horses nowadays, but in the sense that they were almost constantly being pursued or sought after by marauding carnivora and it was policy to keep an eye on either side of the head, particularly if it could also see something of what went on behind.

As a result of this semi-lateral or oblique eye positioning the horse is able to view two separate pictures at the same time; one on either side of its body.

A line carried through the centre of each eye of a Thorough-bred horse would lie at an angle of 35 to 40 degrees with another drawn longitudinally through the centre of the head and neck. In a Shire horse the angle would be between 40 and 45 degrees. This means that the Thoroughbred sees more of what is happening in front of it than the Shire, but the Shire may see more of objects on either side.

Either horse by a slight effort (greater in the Shire) can converge both eyes to focus simultaneously upon something a little distance in front of its head. At the time it does this, both ears will automatically prick forward.

When a horse of any breed is paying close attention to the lateral view – the objects on either side of the body – it cannot simultaneously obtain a very useful view of those in *front* of the body, and in like manner when its ears are pricked and it is staring straight ahead it will be incapable of seeing what goes on upon *either side*. (Fig. 8.)

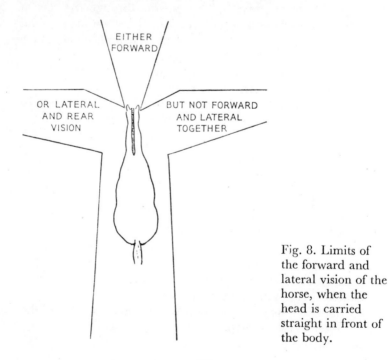

EITHER FORWARD

OR LATERAL AND REAR VISION

BUT NOT FORWARD AND LATERAL TOGETHER

Fig. 8. Limits of the forward and lateral vision of the horse, when the head is carried straight in front of the body.

Fig. 9. Heads of an Arab mare (*left*) and a Thoroughbred pony (*right*), showing eye placement. Note the wider forehead of the Arab and the greater space between the eyes.

Fig. 10. A comparison of the eye placement in (A) a Thoroughbred with that of (B) a Shire Horse.

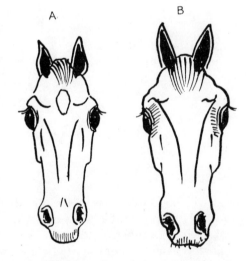

Although the degree of ability to see objects behind the body will vary with the position the eyes occupy in the head, whether they are set at 35 or 45 degrees for example, most horses can obtain *some* degree of posterior vision even when the head and neck are carried in a straight line with the rest of the body. It is evident, however, that a streamlined Thorough-

Fig. 11. Head of a
Heavyweight Hunter
showing eye placement.

Fig. 12. Head of a Shire
Horse showing eye
placement.

bred will be better able to see objects immediately *behind* its
own body than would a heavy draught horse possessing a thick
neck, wide shoulders and prominent hind quarters. Apart
from this, the draught horse would possess a considerable
advantage on the score of eye placement and often of what is
known as *proptosis*, the degree of protrusion of the cornea
outside the margin of the space bounded by the eyelids, which is
usually more evident in the Shire than in the Thoroughbred.

In heavy draught horses, particularly Shires, the dis-
advantage furnished by width of body is somewhat discounted

by the fact that the forehead is also much wider than that of the Thoroughbred and this in itself improves the prospect of seeing objects lying behind the animal's body.

Opposed to this the Shire has increased difficulty in obtaining binocular forward vision since its forehead is wide and there will be greater difficulty on this account in converging or focusing both eyes simultaneously upon objects ahead. (See Figs. 9, 10, 11 and 12.)

But all kinds of horses and ponies are able to view objects at all points of the compass and to observe the approach of man or other animals from every direction so long as they are grazing with mouth to ground. In this position the eyes can see between any pair of the horse's limbs, the only factor limiting the range of their vision being the closeness of the horizon when viewed from this position. (See Fig. 5.)

Dogs and other carnivorous creatures follow the movement of possible prey such as a bird or a hare by moving the head, as the degree of movement possible to the eyeballs within their orbits is very limited when compared with that of the human eye.

As a general rule animals keep the pupil of the eye horizontal to the ground whatever the position of the head may be. This would apply to any pupil which was shaped as a transverse slit, but in other instances one might imagine a line drawn transversely across the pupil. It is this line which remains parallel with the ground whatever the position of the head, as a result of the rotation of the eyeball in up-and-down fashion. It implies also that whatever the position of the head the pupil remains central, facing the outer world. The eye does not roll up or down in the orbit so that the cornea – the window of the eye – disappears behind either the upper or lower lids, when the head is raised or depressed.

This does not imply that the horse is unable by an effort of will to achieve this position of the cornea; merely that it does not normally do so when it lifts or lowers the head.

In some cases, however, the third eyelid, the mebrana nictitans, will become elevated and may completely cover the eye. This happens when the eye is inflamed, or irritated by the presence of grit or by a speck of chaff or a hayseed, or when the cornea is touched or subjected to pressure.

In diagnosing the onset of the disease known as tetanus, the head is lifted by placing a hand below the horse's chin. When tetanus is developing the third eyelid shoots up over the cornea and completely covers it, so that only a little of the sclerotic – the white of the eye – remains visible.

The majority of horses have their own favourite position for their head when trotting freely without restraint from reins. But horses are trained to arch the neck, elevate the head and move forward under pressure from the rider's heels until they come up to the bit. When doing this they normally hold the head with its long axis perpendicular to the ground as by so doing they keep their eyes facing directly forward to provide distant vision.

The horse possesses a very useful set of eye muscles intended to turn the eye in various directions, but owing to the position of the eye and the fact that the horse owns a long and very flexible neck, these muscles are not put to a very great deal of use.

Like a lot of animals which possess lengthy necks, the horse finds it more convenient to move the head into a fresh position than to make use of the eye muscles, and, as has already been pointed out, this generous amount of head movement is absolutely necessary in order that the horse may focus its eyes upon neighbouring objects. Even when looking behind the body the horse is apt to turn the head; and the extent to which this is possible is characterised by its ability to flick with its lips a fly off its body as far back as the last rib.

Generally speaking, in most animals frontality of vision appears to be accompanied by increased intelligence. When the degree of frontality varies somewhat in a species the intelligence ratio is usually higher in those individuals which possess it in a greater degree.

This explains why certain breeds of dogs, notably the brachycephalic types, which have almost true frontal vision are almost invariably superior in intelligence to those which possess a semi-lateral vision. I have explained the reasons for this elsewhere. Suffice it to say here that dogs, for example, which are provided with frontal vision, have larger brains, weight for weight, than their long-faced relatives which carry their eyes more laterally. This rule applies also to the equine species for, although horses are not brachycephalic, it is evident even among Thoroughbred horses that the most intelligent specimens are those in which the eyes are set forward or the most centrally on either side of a comparatively narrow forehead. These can be directed immediately upon an object lying straight ahead. The horse can in such a case make use of binocular vision, with both eyes converging upon the object. The head is moved into the position which provides the best possible focus, the ears point forward and the whole operation can be carried out almost instantaneously.

Although the degree of frontality varies so little in Thoroughbreds and depends so much upon the shape and width of the forehead, there may yet be a striking difference in the ease and rapidity with which two horses may carry out this matter of eye convergence, visual reception and automatic response.

In the draught horse and in an unusually wide-browed Thoroughbred, in which the eyes are carried far more laterally, the ears are less active in their movements; and it is clear that ear movement is a good indication of alertness and visual acuity.

In this connection, however, it must be admitted that the two senses, vision and hearing, although complementary, may also be operated without regard the one to the other. For example, blind horses move their ears incessantly to pick up sounds which will indicate the position of objects the eyes cannot see.

During the writer's college days, a bus pulled by a pair of completely blind horses used to travel from Kentish Town to King's Cross and back. Apart from the fact that these horses displayed an amazing degree of ear movement, nobody would ever have suspected their blindness, least of all the passengers. They were guided entirely by messages conveyed through reins and bit, aided by vocal signals between horses and driver; and also by their ability to hear sounds arising from surrounding traffic.

Some of the less highly-strung horses, or it may be those which have not altogether adjusted themselves to modern circumstance and still retain the inherent desire to see what approaches them from directions other than from the front, persist in casting their eyes laterally rather than frontally. While this may be quite all right upon the prairie or even in the marshes, it is no fit way to behave when a horse is racing at a furious pace upon the flat or when seeking the easiest way to approach a jump.

Modern horses have no need to be constantly on the look-out for predatory animals creeping up on either side. They have to focus their eyes and their attention upon what lies ahead, at fields and fences; and the ability to do so is nowadays more apparent in our modern Thoroughbreds than in horses of coarser blood.

But occasionally one encounters the racehorse which loses one or two lengths in a race by permitting its attention to wander to the crowd or to other horses when it should be looking straight ahead. Some trainers now overcome this tendency by the use of blinkers, and many horses which have failed in previous races have succeeded in winning subsequently when their ability to do a little side-gazing on the way has been curtailed by this means.

Lt-Colonel Tom Nickalls, writing in the *Field* of June 27th, 1963, asked whether blinkers worn on a racehorse constitute a rogue's badge, or not. He mentions that Crocket, by King of the Tudors, won five races and was rated the best colt of 1962. He never wore blinkers. In 1963, although first time out he won his race in moderate company, he showed unwillingness to give his best. In the Two Thousand Guineas Crocket gave up after three-quarters of the distance and refused to race. In his next race, the St James's Palace Stakes, he wore blinkers and won pulling-up, by six lengths.

Other horses may run a race well in blinkers, then subsequently behave wretchedly in them. What is the cause? In the first place there is of course no evidence as to why Crocket, or for that matter any other horse, should run consistently on any day. There may be a number of other operative causes apart from visual inattention. Even human beings, keyed up to win by zeal and ambition, are not always able to do their best.

But horses have other problems to contend with. A great many racehorses have already experienced or are in the process of competing with spinal pain arising from arthritis and spondylosis of the spinal vertebrae, as I have already shown in *Horses in Action*.[1]

Others may be suffering from cardiac dysfunction, digestive or other troubles. We, ourselves, are often handicapped by what we term a 'bad heart', or even by a cold or other virus infection. Horses undoubtedly suffer from all of these disabilities, often without manifesting any other marked symptoms, so it would be unfair to judge the value or otherwise of blinkers without details of a large number of examples, based upon many horses, their previous history and their success or otherwise when blinkers were worn.

Mares and fillies suffer at times from the disabilities peculiar to their sex and this is more manifest in Spring and early Summer, but some mares show such irregularities at any time of the year.

It might be worth while to ascertain what part, if any, width or narrowness of forehead plays in the ability or the willingness to win a race.

The wider the forehead, the greater is the distance between the eyes, and the less the degree of visual frontality with a greater tendency to gaze upon either side of the course instead of converging both eyes upon the ground ahead. If lateral vision is occluded frontal vision must take its place. No horse is likely to gallop at its fastest speed unless it can see clearly where it is going. Head shape and eye placement in the Thoroughbred is a subject deserving of far more study than it has already received. (Figs. 9 and 10.)

The question is often asked: *How far* can a horse see? It is not, of course, only a matter of how much it can see, but how well it may see it and what it may be able to *recognise* at any given distance.

In the horse, as in other animals, very little information

[1] Published by Country Life, 1963.

may be conveyed to the brain from images of objects which remain perfectly still. As soon as they commence to move they disturb the pattern of the mosaic upon which the horse's eyes are resting and excite attention. Anything which approaches and passes fixed objects in the mosaic is immediately singled out and possibly recognised. The horse, like other animals again, is also interested to discover whether such an object is moving towards or away from it. If away, it may be considered as worthy of pursuit, not for the same reason as a carnivorous animal but merely out of curiosity. If the object is approaching, the horse may 'consider' whether it is something alarming or of no particular consequence; whether to stand ground or bolt in alarm.

Being unable to inquire of the horse how much it sees, one must be content with considering the evidence provided by animals concerning their individual acuity of vision.

It seems likely that a horse sees most and farthest when it stands still with head erect and with the forehead and muzzle held perpendicular to the ground.

Herein lies the chief difference between horse and dog in their relationship with the outer world. The dog continues to focus much as we do, changing the curvature of the lens of the eye by compressing or releasing its elastic body within an enclosing capsule. This is made looser or tightened through the varying pull exerted upon it by the ciliary muscle.

The horse possesses this mechanism, but makes little or no use of it, mainly because its ciliary muscle is not very effective and it finds it more simple to focus its eyes by moving its head into the position which enables it better to see the object in which it is interested.

We must remember also that horses have not a great ability to concentrate their attention for any length of time. If a sight is alarming, the horse responds immediately by retreat. If it does not prove alarming it is of little consequence and so is not worth looking at. Jumps are a different matter entirely. The horse is quite aware, even if sometimes its rider forgets, that it is not a natural jumper and that the safe negotiation of obstacles depends upon looking – and learning. Most horses give jumps, therefore, their full attention. There are a few who fail sometimes to keep this necessity in mind, and, in addition there are a great many who are just not interested. (Plates 1, 2 and 3.)

When a horse, one that is trying, approaches a jump, it does so with head raised to the most suitable level, both eyes converged forwards upon the obstacle, and both ears sharply pricked – a sign of concentration. On the way towards it the horse has to sum up the height and nature of the jump and the diminishing distance between itself and the jump as the seconds fly by. (Figs. 13 and 14.)

Fig. 13. Diagram showing the stages of a jump.

It has to time matters so that it reaches the jump, standing on its legs and with its paces continuous. In other words there must be no obvious check in the horse's progression between setting off at the jump, landing and moving off again on the opposite side of the fence.

This implies that the number of paces the horse takes needs to be varied at each jump so that when it arrives with head four feet from the jump, its body and limbs will be in the exact position for the take-off.

There is one slight snag with which every horse has to compete, although its rider has no trouble at all in this respect. It is that when the horse is four feet from the jump, which is approximately at the second of taking-off, it can no longer see it. Many refusals result from this cause, when at the last moment the horse loses sight of the obstacle.

There are a number of reasons for this. The first is that the horse carries a broad forehead and a long wide foreface. The eyes are perched a little obliquely on either side of the foreface so that at any time it requires a little effort to induce them to look forward and not sideways.

Fig. 14. An impression of a horse landing from a jump. Note the position of the left foot, coronet and fetlock, and the strain thrown upon the tendons and ligaments at the back of the cannon.

To get the best view up to this moment the horse has carried its head high and in this position it is no longer able to look downwards at the jump with both eyes, since the wide muzzle and nostrils obscure the view.

At the four feet range binocular vision, so far as the jump is concerned, goes completely out of action. If the horse wants another glance at the jump it must tip its head slightly to one side and view it with one eye only.

Not only does the horse, when approaching the jump at speed, need to measure the height to the top of the rail or uppermost layer of bricks or blocks, but it has also to estimate the total length of the jump, especially in the case of a triple bar or water jump. All this has to be managed with the aid of a ramped retina which can only operate efficiently when the horse has completely free head movement. (See Fig. 6.)

It would seem that horses either estimate their jumps and perform in accordance with their calculations, or they 'jump blind', which means to say that having reached the spot where they think they should take off, they gather themselves for the highest and longest jump they can make into blind space, hoping for the best.

One may wonder how horses 'collected' in dressage order, smart as they may look in the ring with their heads set perpendicularly to the ground, their necks arched and their mouths brought up to the bit by pressure from human leg and heel, ever manage to clear a jump when ridden up to one in this fashion.

The fact is that, if it is to jump successfully, the horse *must* be free to select its own head position to conform with its visual needs. This is something to which very few riders, even the most experienced, pay proper attention.

So many young horses quite naturally take so much notice of unaccustomed noises and sights going on in the world around them that their attention may be distracted from the more important matters lying directly ahead.

This applies especially to those accustomed only to home surroundings where all is quiet and placid. They may suddenly be placed in a horse box – an exciting adventure in itself and enough for one day – carried a short or a long distance and then suddenly deposited in the open again among crowds of horses and people, moving vehicles, flags, brass bands and an artificial arena. Enough to scare the wits out of a young elephant, let alone a three-year-old Thoroughbred.

Every inexperienced horse, however well-trained in other ways, green and unaccustomed to crowds and noises, will enter the ring for the first time looking in every direction other than straight ahead.

The experienced horse, a jumper for example, will have some idea of the purpose for which it is present. It will be summing up the potentialities of the first jump while the novice will be looking around in all directions employing lateral vision on either side with no idea of why it is on the ground at all, or what is expected of it.

All youngsters need education in this way before they settle down to serious business, but it is during these terms of initiation that great harm can be done to their dispositions and temperaments, and this may persist into later life.

Only too often young horses are entrusted to equally young riders who have had little more experience than their mounts. Young horses are in far greater need of good riders, possessed of good hands, good manners and a deal of understanding.

The process of 'breaking-in' the colt or filly must never be left in the hands of the strong but inexperienced rider.

Here, again, some sort of modified blinker, comfortable and soft, may be of use in distracting a young horse's attention from sights not appertaining to the job in hand. The blinkers can be dispensed with when the basic principles have become sufficiently impressed upon the young horse's mind. It may then be better trusted to discriminate between what is important and what is not.

Horses, today, are expected not only to surmount every kind of obstacle human ingenuity can devise, but to do so against the hands of the clock. This necessitates the mapping out of a 'time and work' programme which varies on nearly every occasion, or at every new venue to which the horse is taken. Fortunately, most of the mathematical side of such a problem can be handled by the skilled rider in such events and everything will then depend upon the efficiency or otherwise of the system of communication established between the rider and his mount.

How far does a horse see?

It is likely that with head held reasonably high with forehead and face perpendicular to the ground, in open country the horse will see, when nothing else crosses the field of vision, all the landscape for several hundred yards around by the alternate use of frontal and lateral vision. By careful adjustment of the head the horse might recognise another horse or group of horses a quarter of a mile distant. It must not be imagined, however, that a horse can see a tiny speck on a hillside half-a-mile away, which we might recognise as a man or a woman, and translate it into an enlarged mental image. This is most unlikely as it would require a deal of imagination, and a memory for detail which few animals below the Primates possess.

The horse does not see a landscape as we do. In the first place, being colour blind, the horse fails to see green fields, blue skies and water, and the spring and autumn tints of trees. The eyes of the horse are quite incapable of breaking up the visual image into trees, grass, bridges, gateways, arches, patches of cover and areas of space. It sees the land ahead as a mosaic in shades of grey, including dark areas and a modicum of shadow.

It cannot sort out a grey rabbit from among a patch of green cabbages, unless the rabbit moves – in fact in a landscape free of movement the horse might be unable to sort out anything other than masses forming the greater part of the picture. These would be represented by woods and trees, areas of grassland, or large patches of water, but as all would differ only in tone and not in colour, there is no proof that the horse would have any knowledge as to their exact nature when viewed from afar.

We possess the advantage of knowing that large expanses of green represent grassland. We can distinguish cornland from land growing roots, all by colour shades, but no horse can do this as we can. It must depend for its visual information upon brightness rather than upon colour. It recognises movement by the change of brightness in parts of the mosaic as various parts of the moving object reflect or refract light, as well as upon the changing relationship of the moving body to other fixed bodies.

Nor does the young horse receive verbal or visual teaching from a fond parent who points out objects, gives them a name and explains what they are. The horse knows only what it can teach itself by experience, using mainly the principles of trial and error. Horses learn little by the sense of touch, except perhaps that jumps are hard. They seldom go up to an object and touch it with lips or tongue, neither have they any fingers.

Their knowledge is confined to objects in constant reach such as pails and mangers, rugs and grooming equipment – not a great background upon which to found knowledge.

In the wild state the horse might satisfy its own curiosity. If it viewed a flat grey surface and wondered whether it represented grazing land; or if it saw a patch of brighter grey and hoped it was water, it could find out by approaching it and making a close-up investigation.

With a rider on its back it goes only where the rider wishes.

5. Canadian Cutting Horses giving a display at the Windsor Horse Show. 'The Cutting Horse appears to be able to foresee whatever its opponent may do next.' (See p. 104.)

6. Police horses in action outside the Houses of Parliament. 'Co-operation is entirely voluntary and not brought into being by ill-treatment.'

7. The winner, 'Team Spirit' (*left*), coming over the last fence in the 1964 Grand National, which 'finds horses at their best'. (See p. 110.)

8. 'The whole art of racing is centred upon getting the nose of one's own mount . . . in front of every other nose.' 'Santa Claus' (No 7) winning the 1964 Derby.

5

Hearing

Horses have a very keen sense of hearing and it is likely that, in common with the dog, they are able to recognise a number of sounds well above our own auditory limitation.

Horses hear best when they are thin-skinned with light active ears which move rapidly in every direction. The heavier breeds of horses with thick heavy ears, often nearly filled with hair, are naturally less responsive to sound; moreover, being lethargic as compared with the Thoroughbred, none of their responses is as rapid.

Stabled hunters are able to pick up the sounds emanating from horns and hounds far distant. Some hunters refuse to feed on the day when hounds meet anywhere in the vicinity because, even when their owners hear nothing, they themselves can pick up the sound of the horn and the calls of the hounds several miles away. They will neigh, break out in a lather of sweat and refuse to settle down before nightfall.

Horses of coarser breed will either fail to hear such sounds or will be quite uninterested. They continue to feed and rest while more finely bred horses in the same stable may go nearly mad from excitement.

Quite a number of horses are gun-shy and will pull up instantly if they hear a report. When there is little breeze horses at pasture will be seen to make immediate response even to the report of a gun from over a mile distant.

Hearing is accentuated, of course, when sounds travel down-wind towards the horse.

The apparent ability of some animals to detect the approach of others, human or animal, is frequently misleading to some extent, since many species, including the horse, so often make use not only of their ears but also of vibrations reaching them through the ground travelling up the limb bones and being conveyed through the bony skeleton to the skull and the middle ear.

The proprioceptive sense of the horse has never been inquired into with any degree of thoroughness for reason of the obvious difficulty of arriving at any reliable conclusion.

Nevertheless, any animal as clever in travelling through the air and as placid as many horses are during aeroplane flights must be endowed with qualities which may play a greater part in shaping their temperaments than we are fully aware of at present. Only the exception wrecks the plane.

Any horse with a highly strung, neurotic temperament may become very much affected by the rustling of leaves or paper, the sound of thunder, band music, especially the beating of drums, escaping steam, fireworks and a variety of other noises, which may sometimes only create excitement but at others may give rise to great alarm.

Very little experimental work seems to have been carried out regarding the sense of hearing in the horse, although the subject has come under consideration in a variety of other animals.

While in man the average audible pitch ranges between 20 and 20,000 cycles, Pavlov showed that dogs were susceptible to much higher frequencies, with an upper limit of 100,000 cycles. The rat attained 40,000 cycles.

Owls and some other night birds can detect the supersonic squealings of the mice hiding in long grass and prey upon them. But next to nothing seems to be known about the range in the horse though, as previously remarked, experience of horses stabled during the hunting season encourages one to believe that they hear a great deal denied to human ears.

The horse has also the advantage of possessing a very long neck, movable at every angle, with receptive, concave ears capable of facing in almost any direction. Not only do such ears pick up sounds, but, by virtue of their power of movement, they are able to pinpoint the quarter from which the sound originates.

That horses also appreciate sounds, even those proceeding from humans, became very clear to those of us, who lived years ago among horses when there were still born horsemen in charge of them. The old groom never touched or brushed a horse without producing a continuous hissing between his teeth. The horse listened to this and the inflections of the whistle conveyed meanings, about what the groom was doing and about what he was going to do next. The whistling soothed the horse and established it on terms of friendship with the groom. While the hissing lasted there was no occasion for the horse to worry. A rise in the cadence accompanied each swing of the elbow and wrist as the dandy brush swept through the hairs, or a more measured cadence, softer and more soothing in tone, emerged between the groom's lips while he wiped the eyes and the nostrils and ran the sponge inside the flanks.

The sound not only retained the confidence of the horse but it also expressed that of the groom. There would be no biting or wincing or kicking while that note ran true and the partnership between man and horse retained its honesty.

But the note would change its tone when the horse, bridled and saddled, was stirred up, made to hold up his head, prick its ears and stretch out its limbs to 'stand', while its owner walked into the stable yard to give the horse a final look over before mounting for his ride.

This sibilant hissing of the breath between the teeth was an indispensable part and parcel of the routine of every groom and of every true horseman who spoke to his horse with his voice and caressed it with a hiss.

I often wonder how modern ponies, hacks and hunters get along without it. The only place one hears it now is in a few racing stables and in the occasional dealer's yard which still employ one or two of the old grandfathers of earlier days. The modern young generation have no knowledge of it.

In connection with hissing and horsekeeping the story of the whisperer, now well known, comes to mind. The original 'Whisperer' was an American groom, horseman and wanderer, who came to this country with a reputation that preceded him, indicating that he was able to 'charm' any horse however mean and ill-tempered, into submission, merely by whispering into its ears. In this country he was entertained by various sporting gentlemen who proceeded to make bets as to whether he would be capable of taming a notoriously savage Thoroughbred stallion or whether he would be killed in the attempt.

When approached, the Whisperer readily agreed to be shut in the stallion's yard and box and that the gates should be locked for a specified time. Apparently everyone was quite prepared to help collect the Whisperer's mangled remains, but what really happened when the gates were opened was that the stallion was found sprawled out at full length in the yard with the Whisperer calmly seated on its ribs.

During subsequent years a great many people have experimented in the art of whispering what would appear to be unintelligible sounds to horses – and to other animals – with varying degrees of success and a great many failures.

This does not mean that nobody possesses the power to instil confidence into certain animals and persuade them to enter into co-operation, or at least to lower their resistance towards human approaches. The majority of people do not possess this ability and have to take more drastic means to effect some sort of control and enforce some degree of co-operation on the part of the animal.

Whether in the fortunate few there exists some sixth sense which enables them to find a response in the horse can at present be only suspected. Now that we know that a great many animals transmit electric impulses and possess surface receptors capable of receiving such impulses, another field of inquiry may become established.

Anyone interested in the modulations of the equine voice should listen to the great variety, all in a low tone, conveyed from mare to foal, particularly during the early weeks of life when the foal is receiving tuition from its dam.

The number of different whinnies proceeding from the mare make one wonder why a foal comes into the world with a complete understanding of the mother tongue while a human infant responds to touch better than to the voice and has little understanding of the meaning or intention of speech before it reaches eighteen months of age, and requires another year or so before it can reproduce understandable sounds.

One can learn to distinguish between the whinny which is oft repeated simply to maintain contact and the one which says 'Come closer', or 'Get behind me', when something suspicious comes into view, as well as the quick note, almost a snort, which says 'Pick up your feet and get going'.

The voice of the stallion can be one of the most fearsome sounds, unsurpassed by the roaring of the lion, when the stallion really means business. It is used as a call of defiance and has no similarity to any of the gentler sounds which issue from the gelding.

It cannot be described as a neigh but as a shriek which could hardly be made to sound more fearsome by Satan himself. When accompanied by the thudding of prancing hoofs it is a call to be dreaded, for the Thoroughbred stallion, uncontrolled by bridle or bit, is one of the most dangerous animals alive.

The sound travels for well over a mile and it is intended to challenge any other stallion within hearing, which dares put one foot on the forbidden territory which surrounds the stallion and the members of his harem.

The neutered male – the gelding – and mares live in complete harmony and sexual indifference. Both neigh to each other softly and both whinny. The latter sound is more soprano-like in quality, indicative of kindly feelings between the two, of good fellowship and mutual understanding. Not only does the mare employ the whinny in her ordinary conversation with other horses, and sometimes with her human companions, but she uses it as a greeting early in the morning when one goes out to take up the bedding, feed and water-up.

The mare and gelding appear to have a better repertoire of calls than the stallion, which for all his magnificence tends to possess a one-track mind.

Another musical instrument often brought into the orchestra is known as the 'false nostril'. By rapidly filling this with air, especially that of a cold morning, and instantaneously exhaling it, the horse is able to emit a snort, a loud sound almost peculiar to the species but occasionally employed by other herbivora, especially the bull.

The sound indicates alarm, excitement or sometimes may be only a playful way of making a noise and attracting attention.

Often horses respond more readily to high-pitched sounds such as whispering than to loud, verbal commands – in fact shouting at a horse gets no response other than to drive it away out of sight.

But all of us are aware that the horse can discriminate between a number of sounds made with the human voice, mainly by one person well known to the animal. Often the tone of voice means more than actual words and in fact quite often words mean very little.

Much better response is obtained from nondescript sounds made with tongue and teeth or even by hissing through teeth and lips. The word best understood is some form of 'whoah!' while the old carters employed 'Gee up!' 'Git up!' and similar expressions, many of which had a place derivation and varied with locality.

The fact is that if one can make the horse understand what one requires, the actual form of expression is a secondary consideration. There is no doubt that one obtains closer communion with the horse's brain by limb pressure than by any form of spoken command.

6

The Senses of Smell and Taste

I remember asking a little girl once if she thought horses could smell. Her mother chipped in with the reply, 'Yes! Dreadful!'

Although this was not exactly the thought I had in mind, it must be admitted that horses, and perhaps more particularly their surroundings, possess a somewhat clinging scent, unmistakably their own.

It permeates one's clothing and can only be completely eradicated by a bath and a change of outfit. It must be remembered, however, that in equine circles it goes unnoticed and any attempt to free oneself of it is a complete waste of time. Soon, probably, one begins to like it or acquires an immunity. Few habitués of the stable recognise it and perhaps, after all, there are much more unpleasant smells.

What I really had in mind was the delicacy or otherwise of the sense of smell possessed by the horse and its capacity for sensing the approach of other animals by its aid.

Practically all the air entering a horse's lungs has to pass through its nostrils. Horses are nose-breathers and it is only when a horse is completely exhausted that it drops its tongue, opens its mouth and endeavours to breathe through it. Even then, the horse possesses a large, somewhat pendulous soft palate, which at such time drops down into the pharynx and effectually limits mouth breathing.

This soft palate is also made use of when swallowing water or chewed food and helps to block off the open end of the larynx and avoid choking.

It is apt in some horses to descend quite suddenly into the pharynx during the last stages of a race producing a characteristic rattling or rumbling noise. Operations have been devised to overcome this, but racehorse trainers hold a fixed belief that the noise results from attempts by the horse to swallow its tongue! They endeavour to overcome this by bandaging the tongue into the space between the jawbones, and many claim that the procedure is helpful. Whether such bandaging in any way controls the soft palate's descent or if it maintains an airway between tongue and palate is still undecided.

Nose breathing is very satisfactory in the horse providing the nasal orifice is large, soft and capable of being expanded by the use of muscles during moments when hard breathing is essential.

The size of the openings into a horse's nostrils varies considerably in different individuals. The degree of dilatation possible is greatest in thin-skinned Thoroughbreds and, in these, the variations in nasal diameter give rise to a great deal of so-called 'Thoroughbred expression'.

The false nostril runs upwards as a large blind pouch, but the true nostril, through which air is inhaled, opens into the nasal chambers which contain the very large turbinated bones which are rolled on themselves, covered with mucous membrane and possess the brittleness of egg-shell china.

A very great part of the horse's head is needed for the provision of large air sinuses. Of these, the frontal sinuses occupy the whole of the forehead while the maxillary sinuses cover all the cheek space of the upper jaw above tooth level. The air sinuses fill during expiration, not inspiration.

Apart from these peculiar breathing arrangements the head of the horse could have been quite small, something like that of a lizard, but the horse makes use of his 24 lb of skull as a ballast bob on the end of his long neck. He employs this in pendulum fashion to maintain his balance when galloping and jumping, using an almost rigid body, supported on four props, one at each corner.

The nasal surface in the horse is very extensive and it contains areas of closely packed smell buds and olfactory nerve endings.

A sense of smell is important to enable the horse to find and identify materials which are good to eat and discard those which may be unpleasant or injurious. But whether a horse (or for that matter a cow) is able to detect or suspect poisons or foods which may prove injurious is open to doubt.

Horses standing at covert side have been known idly to pick and nibble the leaves of a yew-tree, the branches of which were overhanging, and subsequently some horses have dropped dead of yew poisoning while galloping at full speed after the hounds. In such cases neither smell nor experience were of any help.

Horses at pasture also sometimes eat ragwort, not infrequently contained within hay, a tall weed with yellow flowers and an unpleasant flavour by human standards. It is not possible of course to decide what horses should like or dislike.

Those which consume any quantity of ragwort are apt to go suddenly mad a few weeks later, dash into walls and become so ill and dangerous that they have to be destroyed.

Others develop unthriftiness and cirrhosis of the liver and end up in similar fashion.

The horse which, in its natural state, lived with a great many other animals in the wilds is able to detect a variety of odours which the wind carries towards it from one direction, but may have no recognition of odours when the wind blows from the opposite direction.

For centuries horses have been credited with a great fear of the smell of blood, but experience leads one to think this is a myth. They used regularly to draw knackers' carts and were employed in *abattoirs*, not only standing in blood but exposed to sights and alarms far more disturbing than mere blood. Some drew trucks containing hundreds of gallons of blood and waggonloads of entrails without turning a hair.

Horses on battlefields were frightened of flame and shells, but took little notice of bloodshed or death, something of which, of course, the horse, in keeping with other animals lower than man, has no understanding or actual fear.

Most horses particularly dislike smoke and flame. Some farm horses show a dislike of entering fields where rakings are collected and burned. Horses usually panic when fire breaks out in a stable and can become extremely dangerous and difficult to handle in such an emergency.

They will eat a great variety of drugs one would expect them to refuse. These include powders smelling strongly of aniseed, or of gentian, nux vomica and even strychnine, which are exceedingly bitter; ginger, and even camphor on occasion. They are very partial to sugary and sweet flavours and will often take linseed oil in their food.

Occasionally one meets individuals which flatly refuses to take any food containing even the most harmless ingredient. These occur more commonly among Thoroughbreds. Heavy draught horses are by no means so particular.

The stallion has an acute sense of smell when a mare is in the vicinity and can decide if one is showing oestrus from a distance of up to 200 yards when the wind blows towards him. Even when securely stabled in a closely fitted loose box, he can detect a mare being brought into the yard. The sound of footsteps does not enter into this as the reception promised by the horse's vocal calls is quite different when the new arrival is of the same sex.

The horse possesses several skin areas extremely sensitive to certain irritants whether in the form of vapour, or solid or liquid. These include the eyelids and conjunctive, the skin surrounding the nasal orifices, the lips and skin of the muzzle. In addition, the skin inside the elbows and groin and beneath the tail, is extremely susceptible to irritants.

Anything objectionable acting upon the skin areas of head and mouth may cause raising of the muzzle and an uplifting of the lower lip, exposing all the incisor teeth. The smell of peppermint sweets will often set this into operation, but it must be remembered that this tooth-baring is a common equine habit, often indicating mere boredom, and is not in any way intended to be aggressive in character.

A similar type of behaviour may make its appearance when the horse smells cake or other tit-bits in a visitor's possession, when it will use the lip-raising posture by way of invitation and when asking for more.

It is difficult to dissociate taste from smell and decide which is the determining factor in the horse. Many horses will refuse a substance (e.g. carbonate of ammonia) by smell alone, while others will accept drugs with a strong smell but refuse them on their taste value. But, as previously mentioned, many horses consume a variety and quantity of evil-tasting medicines mixed with oats and bran, without apparently sensing their presence. These include, in addition to those already named, Epsom salts, saltpetre, iron preparations, quinine (sometimes), various anthelmintic mixtures and others which would be very unpalatable to ourselves.

They have a liking for salt, sugar and honey, but dislike strongly aromatic substances such as eucalyptus, peppermint or thyme, and often turn up their noses quite literally if offered cheese, fats including butter, or anything of a meaty nature.

When short of grass, horses devour leaves from trees, including beech and elm, and have no objection in springtime to a meal of moss, or to fresh bark from a young tree, preferably elm or sycamore, but they are also partial to the bark of plane trees planted along pavements.

They fail to discriminate between plants which are poisonous and those which are harmless. They will steal aconite plants from a garden hedge and die as the result, or will consume hemlock, yew, and ragwort, often with a fatal result.

Being physically unable to vomit the horse can get rid of none of these poisons.

7

Tactile Sensation

Perhaps one of the characteristics which has linked the horse with man is its very acute power of tactile sensation – of skin perception – for it is frequently by means of this characteristic that mental contact can be established between man and horse and horse and man. In order that this partnership between the two can be established it is essential that the man (or woman) should also possess an acute sense of touch and have his or her responses under control. The whole matter of 'hands' depends upon this ability. Some riders are born with 'hands' – others never acquire them.

The horse is also an animal capable not only of suffering but also of exhibiting acute pain, something that many animals fail to do. It is unlikely that there is any suffering in the world so agonising as the sensations experienced by a horse with enteritis, or displacement involving the massive large intestine. Seeing a horse in such agony is something that few people can ever forget.

Mention may be made here of the panniculus muscle, which lies beneath the skin and covers the greater part of the body especially its upper surface. This is the muscle which causes the skin to rattle when the horse rises from the ground, extends all four limbs and shakes its body, in the hope of removing all adhering particles from its skin.

It is the muscle, too, involved in shivering – something the cold horse does with the object of increasing surface temperature of its body and so avoiding chill. When the panniculus contracts the skin wrinkles, as may be noticed in cold weather.

Another use of the panniculus muscle is to dislodge flies and other insects, out of reach of the tail.

While speaking of shivering we should also mention sweating. As opposed to shivering, it is intended that loss of water and heat from the skin shall help to stabilise the body temperature and keep it in the neighbourhood of 100·3°F, which is the horse's normal temperature.

This ability of the horse to sweat at a moment's notice is of the greatest importance in the physiological sense. The greatly increased muscular action associated with galloping produces an instant and marked rise of temperature. This can only be controlled sufficiently by loss of sweat from the sudoriferous glands of the skin. The first result of rise in temperature is an erection of the hairs over certain parts of the body, especially those in connection with the sweat glands of the neck, certain parts of the back and shoulders, the axillae and groin. There are no sweat glands in the skin of the limbs and any apparent sweating from these parts is due to sweat pouring out from the sides of the body and especially from the axillae and skin between the hind thighs.

Sweat pours also, though a trifle later, from all the sudoriferous ducts of the skin and forms a foam on the body and limbs.

In addition to loss of heat through sweating, a considerable amount is lost through the breath which contains water vapour. Unlike the dog, the horse only lolls out his tongue during extreme exhaustion, while the dog uses its tongue as a heat regulator even when at rest. The dog has very little ability to sweat through its skin, other than from between the pads of the feet, but it lets its tongue hang outside the mouth whenever it is running fast or over any distance.

Some horses able to race in this country are unable to adjust their sweat mechanism when exported to lands where they experience tropical heat. They are, therefore, quite useless for racing abroad and a great many attempts have been made in tropical countries to induce them to sweat. The most successful agent appears to be adrenalin or ephedrine, but how racing organisations would look upon such attempts at treatment is not recorded.

Increase of heat production is normally controlled by the nervous system through the motor nerves to the skeletal muscles and through the sympathetic secretory nerves to the adrenal glands.

That horses are capable of responding very rapidly and often very vigorously to skin stimuli is well known to every veterinary surgeon accustomed to administering hypodermic injections to them, into various parts of the body. They find that all skin areas are not equally susceptible to pain inflicted by needle punctures.

The covering of the neck and shoulders is extremely sensitive, the back being less so. This, however, is offset by the fact that it is extremely tough, and veterinary surgeons find as a rule that the skin immediately above the elbow joint offers less resistance to the needle on the part of the horse and, as a rule, the horse shows less evidence of pain when this site is used.

The skin of the lower limbs, often used for nerve-blocking for anaesthesia, is very sensitive, especially around the feet and coronets. The heel at the rear of the pastern is also an extremely sensitive area. In addition to pricks from hypodermic needles causing pain, veterinary surgeons find that horses are highly responsive when there is even slight wounding of the skin below the knee and hock and these are areas very prone to suffer as the result of kicks, punctures and accidental injuries of all sorts.

Most horses appreciate gentle scratching of the skin of the withers and this is often found to be a useful way to make friends with a horse, particularly with an unhandled colt. In the old days when horses were subject to sarcoptic mange, the fact that the horse exhibited great pleasure when the withers were scratched, and also that it made at the same time loud smacking noises with its mouth and lips, was regarded as symptomatic of the disease.

Young horses which object to their heads being handled or haltered, can often be calmed if their withers can be reached and scratched, and the operation continued gradually along the root of the mane until the poll can be reached and handled.

The skin overlying the ribs and flanks of the horse is very sensitive. A saddle which presses down in front upon the bones of the withers *when weight is on the saddle* will cripple any horse and may result in the production of fistula of the wither. Any undue saddle pressure which causes bruising or abrasion will be sufficient to prevent a horse from winning a race or from doing well in a jumping competition.

The fact that a saddle does not chafe the rider is no criterion as to the effect it may produce on the horse. The same may be said for badly fitting bridles which chafe behind the ears and may be too short or too long in their cheek pieces.

Even the most gentle application of the whip over ribs or flanks will produce a type of response different in every horse. Some will fear the whip and may gallop faster when threatened. Others will resent it so much that they will slow down or come to a sudden halt every time the whip is lifted. Some will lash out violently each time the whip descends. The whole object of the whip would appear to be to increase the inherent sense of panic present in most racehorses when galloping at their hardest. In a state of nature horses never exerted themselves to this extent unless they were galloping away from a pursuing enemy. Whether the whip can be substituted in the minds of a few horses as a symbol of an unseen enemy is uncertain, but this may be the case. Usually to increase speed the whip needs to be applied well back, although quite a few jockeys find that 'showing the whip' – a good deal of flourishing with little actual hitting – makes a horse gallop faster than when it is severely whipped. Curiously, striking a horse even lightly on the shoulder may cause *loss* of speed, probably because it disturbs the balance of the forelimb.

While most horses appreciate gentle patting of the neck, gentle stroking of the skin of the neck and face, as well as gentle scratching of the withers with the finger tips, very few regard such fondling as an expression of appreciation on the part of the person engaged in this way. While the dog recognises a connection between the person providing the pleasurable sensation, or appreciates a tit-bit from someone it knows, and is even prepared to repeat some little performance for a succession of tit-bits, the horse does not appear to express or experience any form of gratitude. A horse will not repeat a trick (shake hands, for example) purely in exchange for a lump of sugar, but it may agree to repeat the trick in response always to the same signal, perhaps touching the inside of the knee with the point of the whip. The horse may be taught to respond repeatedly to stimuli, but it does not 'put on a show' merely to gain human appreciation or applause.

Earlier in this book I have made some reference to the delicacy of contact created by the rider's thighs, calves and heels and the way in which pressure applied by the limbs against the saddle flap, or directly on to the horse's skin, may effect complete understanding and a degree of control over the horse by the rider.

This two-way current of meaning and response becomes in some instances a little beyond what can be ascribed to purely physical contact, and a great many observers have felt sure that in selected cases the degree of thought transfer can only be attributed to the existence of a sixth sense – telepathy. Such a matter is a little beyond the scope of this book, but I feel it should at least be mentioned as a possibility. (See Chapter 9.)

Contact between man and horse is established largely through touch and hearing as well as through vision. The horse watches the owner or rider the whole time, even to some extent when he is mounted, although it may not appear to be so doing.

The horse was not shaped as it is in order that it might conveniently carry a man. It simply happens that the back of the horse fits comfortably into the seat and thighs of a person when in the saddle or seated on its back. In many instances the fit is so perfect that the horse and rider may seem as though fashioned all of a piece.

It so happens that the horse's withers and the portion of the back posterior to them, together with the skin covering the ribs, are most sensitive to touch. As a result primitive man and primitive horse must have shared a common sensation engendered by the contact of their respective bodies, aided by the appreciation of movement conveyed to the rider through the body of the horse.

Unfortunately for the succeeding generations of horses some man, who was possibly not a very expert rider, invented stirrups, and the idea was taken up by those who wanted not only to use the horse as a means of getting from one place to another but also for military transport. Stirrups needed something solid to which they might be attached and so the saddle came into being. With its use the intimate contact between horse and man was diminished, to be replaced by a cruel mechanism which pinched the spine and raised sores and sitfasts on the skin.

Even today too little attention is paid to the pattern of the saddle, its correct fitting and upkeep. Probably no human being can estimate the acute discomfort, even severe pain, suffered by so many horses as a result of badly fitted saddles. Unfortunately, the saddle does not pinch the rider's posterior in the same way that it pinches the back and withers of the horse and accordingly few riders pay heed to the fit or condition of a saddle until the horse has developed injuries which render it unfit to ride.

But we are writing now of extremes, and conditions such as have been described should never arise in horses owned by intelligent persons who have any understanding of the horse or its welfare.

What I would like to stress is the amount of 'conversation' – exchange of ideas – which may take place between horse and rider merely through the medium of skin pressure.

I am confident that the intelligent horse (and it must be remembered that as far as the *senses* are concerned, the horse is far more perceptive than its rider) is capable of reading every thought which enters its rider's mind concerning the matter in hand and is able to sense every intention, share every thrill, every spot of fear, doubt or loss of confidence, which passes through his or her consciousness. It transmits back through the same skin medium, as much as by its actions, its own sensations and feelings to exactly the same extent as it reciprocates the rider's intentions, hopes and doubts.

We have been discussing natural transmission; we must now consider transmission of contact through an artificial medium.

Probably the most direct and most urgent connection of this kind existing between horse and man is conveyed through the bit and reins. While contact between the skin of horse and rider is sensitive and *mutual*, that conveyed through the bit is apt to be a more one-sided affair since it may cause pain within the mouth of the horse without creating any corresponding sensation in the hands or wrists of the rider. In fact, such pain is only caused to the horse when the rider is rough-handed, thoughtless or ignorant, a description which fits, unfortunately, by no means a small proportion of those who handle horses today.

When the rider is better equipped, when he, or she, possesses what can best be described as 'hands', the interchange of communication between the two will be painless, and even appreciated by the horse, while the response made by the horse to the bit, induced by the hands of the rider, may give rise to a degree of pleasurable understanding to both.

It must be admitted, however, that while riders frequently lack 'hands', horses equally often lack 'mouths'. The fault lies in this case nearly always in early training. Insufficient opportunity is afforded the young horse to get used to the 'feel' of a bit in its mouth.

Today things are done in a hurry. The real horsemen of days past used to allow their youngsters to wear soft rubber bits, followed by one 'improved' by the addition of 'keys'. After this, frequently months later, the colt was driven daily on 'long reins' along the then untenanted roads, until it responded to gentle handling and had developed a mouth.

One seldom made any attempt to 'back' a young hack or hunter until it responded freely to bit and reins and had become used to carrying a 'dumb jockey'. Not uncommonly the colt was trained to carry a weight on its saddle before being ridden. Fifty years ago it would have been led daily on the roads beside another mounted horse, bitted and reined and saddled, with a heavy bag of sand strapped firmly on the saddle, until it had become used to carrying a weight on its back.

Today there is little time for such performances. The man who would willingly dally for a few weeks running in a new car before trying it out at speed, would grudge similar time spent on mouthing and training a young horse.

If young horses were habitually bitted on soft material until their gums had acquired the necessary degree of hardness, the number which would eventually emerge with perfect 'snaffle mouths' would be much greater.

Bad hands demand bad bits, it would seem. The amount of unnecessary hinged ironmongery inserted nowadays between the tender gums of green horses indicates that such animals have never been accustomed during early life to bits which cause no pain. The only other reason is that their present riders may be devoid of the 'hand sense' and have two ideas only in mind – 'full speed ahead' and 'stop'. The stop is effected by pinching the tender jaws between metal levers and chains until the pain becomes sufficiently excruciating to remove from the horse's mind any desire to proceed a step farther in any direction.

When this kind of riding is accompanied by a marked ability to kick one's heels into the horse's ribs on every possible occasion, or to puncture the overlying skin with spurs until it bleeds, riding horses become divided into two main classes: those properly ridden and handled, which enjoy their labours, and those which do everything in pain and under compulsion, putting up as much resistance as they dare.

Harking back to control exercised through reins and a bit, my own mind travels along the lines of the simple snaffle rather than along complicated double bits and headpieces with martingales of all kinds which exert leverage but lessen the delicacy of contact in all but a minority of hands.

But whatever the type of bit, no horse can possess anything approaching 'a mouth' unless it has a good forehand and is able to carry its head at a suitable height without boring in an attempt always to get its head down. The collected horse is for ever riding on the bit and can be kept there by gentle heel pressure and controlled by the lightest of hands.

The horse that pulls constantly may be a hereditary puller, a rebel by nature, or it may have had its mouth repeatedly jagged by novice hands in its youth. Sometimes a horse with tender gums discovers that it suffers less pain when it takes hold of the bit or carries it in the angle of the mouth (rather than upon the jawbones) than when it allows it to be controlled by even a gentle hand. Too little attention is paid to the fitting of a bit or a saddle. Although heredity, bad conformation and bad temper may be blamed occasionally for the fact that so few horses possess good mouths, a great deal more should be attributed to bad 'breaking', not allowing a young horse to wear a mouthing bit for some considerable time and the fact that the breaker himself 'has no hands'.

Children are often given their first riding lessons by persons who cannot ride. They may even be encouraged to regard their ponies as status symbols rather than as living sensitive creatures differing entirely in their natures from their now discarded cycles, which responded to energetic treatment but possessed no feelings.

Sufficient time is seldom spent in teaching young children the meaning and importance of 'hands' and in impressing upon them that bits are hard metal objects which compress the sensitive jawbones of a pony and cause intense pain.

Perhaps (with the permission of the parents, of course) it might be a useful practical lesson if children, bits-in-mouth, could be 'ridden' by other children until they learned how a bit feels when another child is manipulating the reins. Nothing short of practical experience can ever get into a child's mind the pain that can be caused by senselessly dragging and yawing upon a bit inescapably fixed between a pony's jaws.

Now that competition at gymkhanas and club meetings is so keen among young children who lack suitable training either in the control of their ponies or of themselves, a great amount of cruelty is caused to their much abused mounts, sometimes quite unwittingly. But there is another aspect to consider.

Even to children truly in love with their ponies there is an ever-present risk of injury and danger when they are permitted without careful supervision and control to caper about amid and upon what, after all, can only be regarded as primitive and potentially dangerous little animals. The annual number of accidents and deaths among children from such causes is mounting and, even if it seems unnecessary to warn parents to exercise caution and to watch over their children, and, even if such advice casts a shadow upon a page of a book which deals with horses rather than children, it will be well worth while if it saves only one child each year from serious injury, or worse.

8

Equine Emotions and their Indications

Out of all the animals with which man comes into contact it is likely that the horse is the one most capable of registering what is going on in its own mind. Being an extremely highly strung animal it not only expresses its emotions very obviously, but it is also capable of a rapid change in the character of those emotions and is no less quick in expressing them in a way which most human beings can interpret.

What is particularly extraordinary concerning a creature so emotional as the horse is the fact that it should also be so adaptable, so capable of suiting its moods to those of its master or mistress.

It is remarkable also that whereas in the wild state it recognised only its own kin and made no friendships outside its own family circle, in a state of domestication it 'pals up' with animals of an entirely different kind, even with species only second in emotional instability to the horse itself. The stable cat, the goat, the Dalmatian dog have all been recognised as the inseparable companions of individual horses in years gone by.

The mental equipment of the horse is, of course, quite incapable of imagining anything at all resembling the muddled emotional upheavals which beset the human mind, but among all animals it is closer to humanity in the part which emotion plays in shaping the course of its domesticated life. One may regard the horse as having rather more of a 'one-track mind' than the dog, for example, since the dog has a greater variety of associations within the circle of its human companions, and a far wider range of interests.

Like the horse, the dog can change quickly from one emotion

to the other. But the dog appears to accept humanity for what it is, with all its faults, its frailties and its inconsistencies, while the horse still expects the human creature to behave in rational fashion and continues to exhibit surprise when the creature does something quite contrary to equine expectation.

It is reasonable to suppose that the average horse, normally a gregarious animal, finds in man another animal unadapted to a solitary existence, and is willing, for want of something better on four legs, to accept a human companion as being the next best thing; especially when as so often happens, the human companion is eager to accept the horse in preference to another of his or her own kind, and provide it with board and lodging.

The horse, always in need of leadership, recognises, perhaps, that the human mind has attributes lacking in itself, greater initiative and the ability to make life interesting by frequently modifying the patterns of normal behaviour.

Some horses appear to possess a certain sense of humour and are prepared also 'to act daft' occasionally in order to pander to the whims of humanity.

But what starts as fun may gradually develop into a liability. The horse has a propensity for learning through the influence of what may be regarded as a series of conditioned reflexes. In consequence it develops by stages from being man's playmate to man's plaything, which is somewhat different.

Incidentally being a plaything is far more exacting and entails in many instances sacrifices on the part of the horse greater than it may feel inclined to make.

The horse normally displays its emotions in a variety of ways. It possesses very 'speaking' dilatable nostrils which quiver, expand and contract, registering interest, suspicion, fear or even on occasion a fit of temper.

The size, thickness and relative weight of the ears differs vastly in individual horses. They are smaller in blood horses and in most of our indigenous ponies, particularly as most of these have been crossed recently with Thoroughbred blood. Some ears tend to loll sideways, but in the alert, well-bred horse they prick sharply forwards at any sound and in addition they do this every time the eyes are focused ahead, in binocular vision, upon some object in the foreground. Ears directed backward upon the neck indicate either temper or great resolve, as during a hard-run race. In the case of a brood mare, with foal at side, it is good to keep well out of her way when her ears take a backward turn.

There appears to be a sympathetic connection between ears and nostrils. Usually when the former prick, the latter dilate, and in many cases where excitement plays a part the horse snorts violently through the nostrils, the ears pricking forward on each occasion.

Another instance of co-operation is during the gruelling stages of a race. When 'the heat is on' the nostrils dilate widely and the ears are frequently laid back upon the neck, coming forward again when the pace is relaxed and when pulling up after the race is over.

Moving up to a jump the nostrils are usually widespread and the ears carried well forward as the eyes spy out the lay of the land.

One must always view with suspicion the horse which moves off after being mounted, with ears laid back, as this usually implies the intention to buck the rider off at a suitable moment.

It would seem that when the whole attention is devoted to speed, ear movements cease, apart from their often being carried backward. This does not then imply that the horse is in any way annoyed at having to gallop, but is resolved to give of its utmost. A horse galloping in a flat race among a group of others with its ears cocked forwards is seldom putting on a great effort, for, as already mentioned, the ears invariably lie backward during moments of extreme stress. In such cases it appears that the animal is determined to put on a great speed in spite of physical distress or discomfort.

The tail also expresses the emotion of the moment in certain instances, usually when the horse is more or less at its ease. During a gallop the tail may occasionally be swished but more usually it is forgotten and follows on behind in a curve or a straight line.

The horse, well and active, will carry its tail high and proudly arched at the dock so that the hairs swing clear of the hind limbs. This graceful arching of the tail was admired many centuries ago and is ably characterised in many old prints, and even in many of the prehistoric cave drawings.

Mares more particularly, especially those of the 'squealer' type, will bury their tails closely into the space between the buttocks. Coupled with backward directed ears, this implies a distinct tendency to lash out with the hind feet.

Sweating has already been discussed. It will suffice here to repeat that horses sweat from excitement or fear and that few horses gathered on a racecourse will be free from patches of sweat on the neck and body, while those more highly strung may sweat profusely, in some cases the drops will run down the limbs and collect as foam.

Body surfaces also vary in different horses according to the season of the year, the amount of grooming and general condition. In spite of this a great many jumpers and steeplechasers appear very dry in coat and even very poor in condition and yet win hard races. As a general rule, however, no horse can be at the peak of fitness until it has cast its previous coat entirely and is in good smooth shape again. This applies also to breeding stock, for no mare is likely to conceive before she has cast her old winter coat and come out in her full pristine beauty.

The eyes of a horse are not only very beautiful but exceedingly expressive. They are capable of conveying a great deal of information to anyone familiar with the horse as to the mood and inclinations of their owner.

We hear of a kind eye, a round full eye, a 'mean' eye – a term imported from across the Atlantic – or we may be told that a horse 'shows the whites' of its eyes. It may do this because the space between the lids is large and the cornea cannot bridge the gap. As a consequence some portion of the white sclerotic coat becomes visible.

One is always taught to regard such an animal as a rogue, apt to be treacherous, willing to throw you and trample upon you if given the chance. So far as personal experience goes there is little basis for this suspicion, providing that all other portents are normal. If such a horse were in the habit of laying back its ears, squeezing its tail tight against its hind quarters, emitting a shrill squeal when approached or touched, one might anticipate trouble whatever the condition of the eye.

But when the eye alone is involved, showing a lot of white, horses may be excellent performers in the field and determined gallopers. Such a horse is rarely a slug. If this kind of eye has a fault, it is probably because it allows the horse to see too much, more perhaps than its brain can accommodate. It is likely that this eye condition is not the real reason for impaired temperament. It may well be a case of giving a horse a bad name; then counting up its faults.

I have known one horse, at least, which showed the whites of its eyes and was particularly reliable and remarkably good across country. Another, with the same fault, would endeavour to cowkick me as soon as my foot reached the stirrup in the act of mounting. There is no proof, of course, that this conduct was in any way associated with the eye condition.

This must not be confused with 'wall eye' in which there is lack of pigmentation of part or whole of the iris, with sometimes similar loss in the skin of the face near the eyelids, or of the eyelids themselves.

Wall-eyed horses are not popular, but they are often also parti-coloured and such horses usually make good saddle-horses, so there is probably no association between wall-eye and bad temper or unreliability.

The only other characteristic concerning the eye we need consider is what is known as 'stargazing'. The horse which indulges in this habit carries the head at a high level, is uncomfortable to ride and difficult to control with reins. Many of them pull and few have any 'mouth'. Such horses may be 'cured' by the use of a standing martingale, but they will strongly resent this and may be thrown badly off balance, so much so, sometimes, as to be unsafe to ride.

One may be inclined to wonder whether this tendency to carry the head high depends upon defective shape of the fundus – the back of the eye – resulting in inability to focus unless the head is raised to this position.

In freedom, and to a more limited extent in domestication, horses express emotion by changes in their vocal calls. The scream of a stallion is a really terrifying sound especially when heard during darkness on an otherwise silent night. The whinny of a mare to her foal is by contrast sheer music in pianissimo. The shrill neigh of alarm, alerting a dozen other horses at pasture, is entirely different to either of the foregoing. The peal of music which floats across a field when one approaches its gate early in the morning carries a welcome nobody could mistake.

The 'squealing' mare has a tone of her own also, but this usually arises from ovarian disease or irregularity, and as such it can hardly be included among calls signifying natural emotions.

Everyone who keeps a horse, or grows up with one, will agree that the range of sounds which may proceed from the equine larynx is very extensive, and that the meaning of most of them becomes clear to one who constantly listens to them.

That horses, like many other animals, hold conversations among themselves cannot be disputed, nor that horses can vary the sounds they make in order to express their emotions, or their feelings at any particular moment. It must not be imagined that such conversations are prolonged or very descriptive, for the brain of the horse is not sufficiently well developed to contain many ideas at any one time.

On rare occasions horses may possess characteristics, worthy or otherwise, which are not evinced by any outward manifestation of their own making.

A recent advertisement in a journal devoted to horses and their owners, read as follows:

> '*For Sale*. A 15.2 h.h. genuine hunter gelding. Not a novice ride and carries a bit of red in his tail.'

Obviously, one would gather, not the sort of horse to be popular at a crowded meet, and yet one that might possibly give a good ride across country when once 'on its own'.

One may speculate concerning the mentality of a horse deserving this description. Does he show the whites of his eyes?

Is he naturally vicious, sadistic or anti-social? The Americans would probably summarise it by saying he was 'mean'.

But need a horse carrying a bit of red in his tail necessarily be any of these things? He is quite obviously suspicious of anything which approaches him from the rear. Perhaps he lacks rear vision owing to the position his eyes occupy. Maybe when a youngster he sustained some injury or was attacked from the rear. Perhaps his endocrine glands are at fault.

It would seem likely that even in the absence of the bit of red, the knowledgeable members of the hunt would have observed how tightly he kept that tail tucked into his rump and given him a wide berth. But once decorated in this way he is branded for ever as a rogue – and not a novice ride!

Before one can judge such a character it would be well to observe his behaviour in a loose box or when tied in a stall. If he kicks out at the person who approaches to groom or feed him he is a rogue indeed.

Among a great many of the indigenous ponies running semi-wild on our moors and hillsides, this habit of lashing out at human beings with both hind feet is becoming very common, especially among ponies which are able to approach road edges. Apart from the risk of these ponies causing car and motor-cycle accidents, there is another danger. It is quite common on the Dartmoor roads and in the New Forest for motorists to pull up their cars on some waste ground near the highway and eat a picnic lunch or tea. The ponies are used to this and at once importune the travellers for tit-bits in the form of sugar, cake or biscuits. All goes well while the supply of food lasts, but immediately it shows signs of running out it is not unusual for a pony which has been fed to whip around and let out with both hind feet at his benefactor.

Every year people with kind hearts but little knowledge of the working of the equine mind get kicked, sometimes severely, in spite of the many notices posted around asking visitors not to feed the ponies. The authorities fear that the animals may be encouraged to approach and stray on the roads.

Local inhabitants know quite well of this other risk to people who feed them.

Among their own species injuries from kicks are not so common as one might expect, but the moors are becoming invaded by various kinds of interlopers and the ponies are steadily becoming fewer. From their early days ponies learned that their companions can kick as fast and as hard as they themselves can, so that the game is hardly worth the candle when reckoning up the kicks received in return.

But ponies regard motorists as easy game, people who never kick back.

With reference to the matter of appetite and a liking for tit-bits, I have heard parents say that, when they buy another pony for a growing son or daughter, they will insist upon obtaining one of the 'always hungry' kind. The reason appears to be that with the other kind of pony, every time the son or daughter is tossed over the pony's head, panic reigns if the pony returns home alone. One of the hungry kind, however, immediately puts its head down to graze and the erstwhile rider may then catch and remount it without difficulty – if still in a condition to do so.

The pony is also much easier to catch when it comes trotting towards a pail containing a handful of corn than when it capers madly around the field available to nobody other than a cowboy swinging a 40-foot lariat.

A little applied psychology has its uses when we keep animals as pets, we are apt to misunderstand their motives for behaviour. What we must always remember is that we are a sentimental race where animals are concerned and we tend to practise anthropomorphism – a big word which, when interpreted, means: We accord to our pets the manners and behaviour we would *like* them to exhibit, and we are apt to disregard the fact that in spite of the adoption of an artificially pleasant façade, the morals and manners of a domesticated animal will always be those with which it was endowed by nature.

9

Extra-sensory Perception

One of the forms of perception common to most animals, and seldom discussed, is known as the *proprioceptive sense*. Because we humans possess it, or perhaps for that very reason, we seldom realise that both in ourselves, and in particular in such active creatures as the horse, it controls a great many of the bodily movements and their synchronisation.

Throughout the body, nerve endings situated in various parts such as the limbs, mouth, eyes, nose and ears, convey messages to the animal's mind concerning all these parts and their relation to each other, as well as to space, even when the parts of the body concerned are completely outside the animal's line of vision. This proprioceptive sense is especially important in the horse and other quadrupeds which gallop at speed over all kinds of surfaces, for every one of these animals must possess accurate knowledge regarding, for example, the whereabouts of its hind feet, which it is quite unable to see. This applies to every phase of movement during such complicated activities as galloping among other horses, balancing itself around corners, jumping over obstacles, or even during more simple operations such as lying down and rising from the ground.

No doubt most of us have at some time or other watched trick horses in circuses, or maybe occasionally in gymkhanas, picking their way between jars or bricks laid haphazardly upon the ground, stepping accurately with the hind feet as well as fore in the interspaces, without ever knocking one of the obstacles over. This seems even more remarkable when one recollects that the horse is completely unable to see its hind feet and that in the four-legged animal the feet do not work on the principle of the four-wheeled vehicle, in which the rear wheels must go where the front wheels lead. All this degree of accuracy is dependent entirely upon the proprioceptive sense which enables the horse to associate in its mind the relationship between fore feet and hind, and to retain in its consciousness an accurate perception of exactly where each fore foot landed, and transmit this to the nerves and muscles controlling the unseen hind feet.

We are so used to seeing this kind of activity, and even indulging in others of a similar nature, that it never occurs to us to realise how intricate a mechanism is involved in the execution of even simple locomotory activities. When we realise that a foal is born wet and helpless and that sometimes within an hour or two it is on its feet and even galloping behind its mother without any help or teaching, we may begin to understand the manner in which this 'built-in' proprioceptive sense makes it possible for young animals to survive when living in a state of nature, and dependent for survival upon their ability to get on their feet and make themselves scarce whenever predatory animals are on the prowl.

Four-legged animals do not make use of the sense of touch as we do, as they lack hands, and the nearest example to the proprioceptive sense in ourselves is illustrated by the knowledge we possess for instance when lying in bed, of the whereabouts of our hips, or knees, or toes and our ability to place a finger with ease and accuracy upon one of them without the aid of a mirror.

The messages conveyed to the brain of a horse through this proprioceptive sense not only inform it whether it is well balanced during a race, or in turning a corner, but also if it is 'right-side-up'. During the course of a jump it enables the horse to decide in flight if it is maintaining its correct relationship with the ground and tells it its actual position in space, and so provides the information which enables the horse to carry out voluntary movements of its head, neck and limbs for the purpose of correcting any errors of which it may by this means be made conscious.

The governing centre connected with the proprioceptive sense is centred in the internal ear. Within this bony casing three semicircular canals and some supplementary membranous sacs are arranged at right angles to one another; these contain fluid carrying calcareous particles in suspension. The canals themselves are lined with nerve endings, coating their surface after the manner of hair. Changes in the position of the animal set up movements dependent upon the laws of gravity within the contained fluids; the calcareous particles impinge upon the appropriately situated hair-like nerves, and the information thus provided travels to the brain which automatically sends motor messages to the muscles governing the movements of limbs and body.

Our own proprioceptive sense not only informs us whether our bodies are resting on the ground or travelling through space, but it also enables us to use our hands and arms, or even our legs and feet, in some measure of co-ordination in order to protect the rest of our body from injury. In addition, it enables us to approximate our hands or fingers in darkness, or at other times when they are out of sight. Owing to our erect stance and to the fact that by a slight inclination of the head we can usually see our feet, we have an advantage over the quadrupeds, who at most times lead with their fore feet and depend upon the hindmost following.

While we can provide a simple explanation as to how a horse is enabled to walk safely and sedately among rows of bottles or bricks, we have as yet no similar explanation concerning the hundred-and-one things a horse may do, any of which may lead us to believe that it possesses senses other than those with which we are all familiar – in other words one may suspect that horses, in common with a number of other animals, possess forms of extra-sensory perception denied to the average human being, even if on rare occasions a few specially gifted individuals lay claim to 'second sight', although none of these so far has ever shown ability to forecast the winner of the Derby in two or more consecutive years.

One is easily led into error, however, in attributing extra sense to animals because some of their recognised senses are so much more highly developed than our own and provide information of a kind of which we can have little understanding. Seeing that the olfactory sense of an almost blind night-flying

moth will provide it with accurate information as to the
location and activities of another moth of the opposite gender
at a distance of a mile, one need not be surprised when a
stallion exhibits an apparently weird knowledge of the whereabouts of a mare on an adjoining farm, not only through its
olfactory sense but, for all that we know, by hearing as well.
The fact that *we* hear very badly must not lead us into believing
that animals generally do not surpass us amazingly in all the
senses other, probably, than touch. In consequence of their
extra sensitivity, horses – Thoroughbreds in particular – are
enabled to sense the presence of possible danger to themselves,
perhaps from an intruder of whose presence or approach we
ourselves would be totally unaware; and they are also capable
of appreciating ground vibrations which mean nothing to the
average human being.

Then again, the horse's reflexes are many times more sensitive than our own and the response to a stimulus is far more
rapid. The finer the breeding the more evident does this extra
sensitivity become, for the reactions of a heavy Shire do not
compare with those of either an Arabian or any horse carrying
a good proportion of Thoroughbred blood. But this does not
fully explain all the unusual things which horses do on occasion,
their refusal to pass certain places and their apparent ability
to detect danger spots beneath the ground on which they walk.

One explanation that may be offered for what it is worth is
their ability to detect electric currents of very low magnitude
and other forms of radiation in much the same way that many
dogs cannot be induced to walk on to some of the seaside piers
which provide amusements. Some of the machines in use
permit the escape of minute volumes of electricity perceptible
to the moist pads of their feet.

Earlier in this book I mentioned a locality in Cornwall
which horses could not be persuaded to pass. When tin mining
was in full swing in that county, it was found that horses
engaged in carting ore from the mines showed a strong dis-
inclination to approaching heaps of ore which contained an
appreciable quantity of certain radio-active rock. Pitchblende,
titanium and uranium ores, years ago regarded as waste,

were particularly objectionable from the equine viewpoint. The fact that the local inhabitants were in the habit of carrying pieces of these radio-active ores in their trouser pockets to charm away warts and cure their rheumatism may be an indication that their radiation output was undetectable by humans, although quite evident to the horse.

With this knowledge at hand today one may wonder whether the hedge in Cornwall which horses refused to pass so many years ago might not have been built from stone derived from local mines which possessed appreciable amounts of radio-active material. In addition, horses are imitative creatures, the result of having lived in droves where one animal gave the signal and the remainder automatically followed suit without exercising their brains to think whether the alarm was genuine or otherwise. Possibly those who stopped to investigate too fully became liquidated and the tendency to dally on the way never became transmitted to posterity.

One must also consider the effect of the illumination of objects in connection with the horse's visual sense and the influence of this upon behaviour. No horse is at all keen to walk into a dimly lit area, or into actual darkness, from an area which is well illuminated, and this at least partially explains why it is often difficult to persuade a horse to enter a horse box unless light enters it at both ends. It also accounts for the fact that during a hunt a horse may flatly refuse to jump a low hedge leading into a dimly lit wood or coppice, even after hounds have already entered it. Unlike cats, which prefer a dim light, and dogs which are equally contented to hunt by day, or at least in twilight, horses are light-positive creatures.

The reason may be that horses are naturally gregarious animals which live on vegetable matter and are classed among those normally hunted by the predatory carnivora. Dogs and cats find their food in dark places, since much of their prey is nocturnal by habit and also inclined to hide among trees and under the cover of foliage or earth. The horse finds its food during the hours of sunlight and takes cover only during the hours of darkness, when one spot is no darker than any other.

There is, however, nothing to disprove and there may be some evidence to encourage us to believe that horses, in company with a good many other kinds of animal, may retain forms of perception which we humans have lost during the course of our evolutionary progress, if that be the appropriate word.

Man is rather remarkable in having undergone a developmental change which other animals have escaped. During some very early stage in his breakaway from the existing Primates his development actually received a check in the physical sense, however one may regard the corresponding changes in man's mental apparatus and all that has happened since in consequence of it. The theory of *foetalisation* suggests that at some early stage of man's biological career the embryo within the uterus of some pregnant ape-woman ceased to develop its usual bodily characteristics and that these came prematurely to a full stop, while the cranium, and the brain within it, continued to grow faster than before.

The body at the time of birth resembled that of an imperfectly developed ape and was similar in development to that of a normal foetus long before its full period of gestation. The cranium and brain, however, increased in size until in the newborn infant it was anything up to two and a half times as large as that of a normal baby ape. However, the cranium developed at the expense of those parts of the skull which contained the centres of sensual perception and it seems possible that man mislaid some of the higher forms – those which we include under the heading 'extra-sensory perception' – and that the horse, the dog and quite a number of other animals retained these, although perhaps not in the same degree as they would have appeared in man had he never undergone the foetalisation metamorphosis.

There is a deal of evidence to lead one to believe that certain animals do make use of powers of perception of which we have no first-hand knowledge, but it is difficult to find proof of this, for we must be careful not to fall into the error of thinking that some of the apparent manifestations may not be capable of some more simple interpretation. It does seem, however that many animals have a weather-sense, or that changes in barometric pressure or humidity act as stimuli to which the animal body makes some definite and salutary response. Also one may sometimes suspect in domesticated animals a sense equivalent to precognition – even after allowing for the fact that they see farther into the minds of their owners than the latter do into theirs. We have to be careful not to confuse their apparent precognition with knowledge acquired from their human acquaintances by virtue of a little clever thought reading.

The best evidence of an animal's ability to foresee an event is shown when it applies to something which no human being could normally foresee. It is even more certain that animals, including horses and dogs, see, or imagine they see, objects, or in some cases whole programmes of activity around them, of which we have no perception whatever.

Some of the apparent behaviour of animals for which we cannot account may be due to the possession of nerve centres in various parts of the body, presumably on the exterior, capable of transmitting electrical energy, and other areas which act as receiving centres. The animal may not be conscious of either transmitting or receiving such impulses until they are interpreted by the brain into conscious messages. This theory is not so far-fetched as it may seem, since we know already that such interchange of electrical impulses occurs in even the more lowly creatures and in these days when the electrocardiogram and the electroencephalogram are everyday instruments in scientific application, the possibility that more use is made of electrical emanation than we are aware of is not beyond the limits of reason.

It is possibly on account of some of these forms of perception that we hear of horses and other animals doing all manner of things which appear strange to us. Quite probably some of the stories which are published are embroidered by the anthropomorphic leanings of the writer, but even when making due allowance for exaggeration and for the possibility of errors in observation, it seems likely that horses, among other animals, manifest, not infrequently, patterns of behaviour which might reasonably be attributed to the possession of faculties or forms of perception of which we, ourselves, have no personal acquaintance.

Strongly tempted though I may be, I do not propose to quote any of the specific instances which have come to my own notice lest I be fallen upon by some of those armchair scientists who know so much about animal psychology, but so little about animals. Although they make use on every occasion of the stock phrase that anything any animal does must never be attributed to conscious thinking, but can always be accounted for by a more simple explanation, they very rarely produce an example when the opportunity arises.

10

Work and Play

Earlier in this book I spoke of the horse as being adaptable inasmuch as it was capable of accepting another animal, as unlike itself as was possible to imagine, as its master and companion. This was a pattern of behaviour which might prove very gratifying to the master, but was, nevertheless, entirely out of keeping with the manner of living for which the horse was primarily designed or intended.

The anomaly is by no means unique in the annals of domestication, for other animals are maintained in captivity in order that they may provide us not with fun, but food. Lower in the animal kingdom we may recollect, too, that ants maintain aphides in return for the sugary juices they secrete or excrete, and equally strange relationships have been found to exist among a variety of wild creatures.

It would be impossible without increasing the length of this volume unduly to discuss the apparent ease with which many horses may be persuaded to adopt an entirely unnatural gait and an artificial mode of progression in response to stimuli emanating from those who ride them.

Many years ago the Spanish Riding School introduced *haute école*, employing for their purpose mainly Lipizzan white horses. These were specially trained to carry out various set movements of a highly complicated nature which became the basis upon which our modern dressage has been founded. These Lipizzaner horses still remain foremost among the exponents of what horses can be taught to do when controlled by reins and harness. Their performance has already been recorded by a number of writers and probably witnessed by many readers, most of whom will also be familiar with the rules and regulations pertaining to the science and art of modern dressage.

The Lipizzaner horses, bred for and by the Spanish Riding School which maintained a number of stallions especially for stud work, were and, of course, still are, comparatively powerful animals of striking appearance. On analysis they reveal in many instances a type of conformation one would not expect to encounter in horses likely to provide a comfortable ride. Instead, it is more adapted to the carrying out of the unusual limb movements demanded, while their heads, necks, shoulders and quarters appear specially designed to favour the specialised muscular development necessary to produce the extraordinary variety of gaits demanded from these horses.

Leaving out any discussion as to the various patterns of *haute école* work and of modern dressage, the feature which more closely concerns us in this volume is that the horse, a creature of the wilds until comparatively recently, as evolution goes, can be coerced not only into collaboration with mankind, but it can be induced to carry out a full programme of locomotory activities so far divorced from anything which nature intended as to be comparable only with the type of regimentation to be witnessed in human circles during the Changing of the Guard. It may be that in the matter of soldiery, officialdom regards goose-stepping and other similar antics as a form of physical exercise essential to the kind of muscular development required during warfare – or it may persist as a relic of the type of barbarism which lay behind the dances and hoodoo of African tribes prior to their emancipation.

However that may be, the case of the riding horse is different. In the English hack or hunter, as in the Lipizzaner horse, this need of selective muscular development does not really arise since the horse, cavorting on four feet, is entirely capable of developing all the muscles it requires for its normal activities without any change in its present conformation, so long as its food supply is adequate in every way.

This fact in itself adds to the surprise one may feel in the knowledge that almost every horse will willingly submit to carrying out unnatural movements at its rider's behest, without putting up any marked show of resistance, and it throws a peculiar light on the mentality of the animal. It must be remembered, however, that such behaviour is almost comparable with what has been achieved in dogs of nearly every type and size in connection with Obedience Training.

The fact that two animals as unlike in so many respects as the horse and the dog should submit to the carrying out of such unnatural performances in order to give some degree of pleasure or satisfaction to their human associates must raise in our own minds the eternal question – Why?

It would appear that man is able only to obtain such complete command over animals which possess one particular type of mentality, not necessarily associated with a very high order of intelligence. The apes can be taught to carry out certain activities in the nature of 'fun and games' merely because they are sufficiently closely related to mankind to possess a sense of the ridiculous and to be entertained by some of the things which would amuse a human child. Although an ape may be taught to wear a uniform, carry a dummy rifle and march, it can never be persuaded to make itself too ridiculous by flexing its joints to their utmost limits, stamping its feet in rhythmic order and spending several consecutive hours marching backwards and forwards between two points only a few feet apart. The ape does only what the ape wants to do. Beyond that it refuses to budge.

The cat, too, is far too intelligent and sufficiently self-supporting and independent to do anything other than cats normally do.

The rat, an intelligent animal, can be taught only to carry out simple operations, usually when it has learned that it is punished by an electric shock if it departs from one established line of procedure.

The horse and the dog are the two outstanding exceptions to those animals whose lives are subject to the law of self-determination, and it is mainly to this that they owe their continued existence.

When one contemplates horses, ridden as they are today with a background of dressage training, and entirely dependent upon the results of human calculation whenever they approach a jump, or trot around a show-ring in a class for hacks, one cannot fail to be the greater impressed by the Cutting Horses of Canada, which are ridden on a loose rein and are able to plan all their moves entirely on their own initiative, or merely with the help of aids provided by the rider's limb pressure, or by the shifting of his weight in the saddle. Next to these gallant little horses come the polo ponies of the world over, which, ridden with only one hand holding the reins and frequently with loose reins, will follow up, turn, twist and pull up from the gallop with a minimum of help from aids.

The Cutting Horse is a descendant of the Quarter Horse and its welfare is ensured by the Canadian Cutting Horse Association, of which Prince Philip is the patron. Some readers may have been lucky enough to have seen demonstrations of this fastest-paced equestrian sport at a number of our country shows during the spring and summer of 1964. (Plate 5.)

I was privileged to ride one of the original Cutting Horses sent over from Canada during 1917, and can vouch for its speed, control and remarkable agility, when ridden freely on a loose rein. This particular specimen, little over 14 h.h., could perform a figure-of-eight at full gallop within a very few of its own lengths, and could gallop in a short circle leaning over at an angle of 35 degrees with the ground without any loss of foothold. It could perform a complete right-about within its own length at a canter merely by flexing the hocks and pirouetting upon its hind feet.

In exhibition Cutting work the steer is gently nosed out from a herd of about fifteen to twenty cattle by the horse, until it is well out in the open. When it seeks to return to its fellows the battle of wits begins, as a cow or even an English steer can perform some remarkable feats of agility in spite of its size and weight. The Cutting Horse appears to be able to foresee whatever its opponent may do next and will lower its head, stretch out its neck and keep nose to nose with the steer and by this means thwart its every endeavour to return to the herd.

By the rules of the game the steer has to be driven about 30 feet clear of the rest of the herd and at this point the rider drops his rein hand, known in Cutting parlance as 'throwing his head away'. From then on the horse moves rapidly, twisting and turning with nose always pointed at that of the steer. The contest goes on for two and a half minutes, when a whistle blows and the horse pulls up and comes again into hand while the points for and against are counted up.

Perhaps the fact should have been emphasised that the horse has proved equally adaptable in another sense, in that it has proved itself capable of being developed by centuries of selective breeding into an animal mentally and physically greatly superior to the stock from which it was originally derived. Man, fascinated by the horse and conscious of all it represented to humanity in the days before he became mechanically minded, took full advantage of this fact, with the result that the stolid, and somewhat sluggish, denizen of the marshes has now developed into a most beautiful creature, brimful of nervous energy, intensely alive and alert. An animal, also, capable of being trained to gallop at very high speed, to struggle on and on, to jump over long ranges of man-made obstacles and to compete with its fellows in a struggle for superiority maintained to the last gasp. Such ability demands a perfect body, trained to the exact degree, neither too much nor too little, coupled with a love of speed for its own sake, the desire to gallop and race not merely on account of pressure from its rider, but as the result of the animal's own volition.

The development of the racehorse, the hunter and polo pony, not to mention the hard-worked children's pony, has been rendered possible only by breeding from those individuals which exhibited another essential characteristic, which we term 'stamina'.

It is not easy to define this word, but in our own minds we can best picture it as indicating great courage, magnificent determination and an ability to accomplish miracles of effort without regard to personal cost.

Horses of many kinds may be forced by pressure applied by a strenuous rider to carry out fast gallops – a feat for which they may have no particular liking. The greatest horse is the one which runs the race from an inborn desire to outpace its rival – the one, too, which carries its rider past the winning post – not the horse which is carried past it only through the energy, or maybe the magnetism, of its rider.

One cannot fail to admire the successful horses of today in much the same way as our ancestors admired the horses of their time, even if we are living in a world in which the speed of travel may attain many hundreds of miles in an hour, while few horses can exceed a 'paltry' three dozen. However, nothing purely mechanical can ever exert the appeal of the modern horse, completely thrilled with the joy of being alive, of being vital flesh and blood, glorying in its own strength and activity, and, by no means least, in its inborn superiority over the machine. All this earns the admiration of mankind.

Such a horse undoubtedly accepts its master as a superior being, a humbling thought in itself. How far the horse is justified in its belief is fortunately a little beyond its comprehension. How long it continues in the belief must depend upon the length of time it proves sufficiently entertaining to its master, but in some respects the horse is more fortunate than other domesticated animals. Even if it descends in the social sense, it will always find people ready to employ it, or even enjoy it, although perhaps in some lesser capacity than previously. The day when the horse was more valuable for human food than for human companionship has gone, with all the horrors that accompanied the traffic in horseflesh.

Although the possession of stamina demands a definite standard of physical development combined with the right kind of temperament, it remains a fact admitted by all who take an interest in the Turf, that horses of all sorts win races, and it would appear that an enormous degree of stamina can sometimes compel a not-so-perfect body to perform great feats of endurance. Whenever such a horse comes into prominence, it owes it mainly to the fact that it is endowed with a superb heart and a marvellously controlled circulation of blood through its arteries and veins. In spite of being handicapped by straight shoulders or weak-looking hind quarters, its circulatory system has proved itself capable of supplying the body with all the oxygen it demands during the course of a hard-run race.

More learned people than myself may write about the exchange of lactic acid between heart and muscles and the ability of the muscles to perform feats of metabolism while actually in action, but we can content ourselves with the thought that without an efficient blood circulation none of these things could happen.

Modern methods of investigation and diagnosis, aided by a combination of the electrocardiogram and the stethoscope, have enabled the veterinary profession to state emphatically that the mechanism of the heart of the horse, the condition, innervation and circulation within the heart wall, are the deciding factors which determine how well a horse can race, if it is so inclined, and how long it can continue to do so.

We may breed horses which possess a certain state of physical perfection so far as appearance goes, but we are not able to guarantee that, because a horse has perfect conformation, it will be provided with circulatory mechanism capable of dealing with the abnormal demands made upon it by mankind. But in spite of the fact that modern breeders aim constantly at higher targets, at producing horses each generation of which shall surpass all the records of the last, the fact remains (if historians are to be believed) that our present-day horses cannot put up performances to equal those of some of the stalwarts of a century ago.

But horses, even the best of them, cannot remain fighting fit throughout the whole of a racing season. As in other types of athleticism peaks of perfection are attained, but it is beyond the power of the body to maintain these indefinitely.

Although this book is concerned with equine mentality rather than with that section of human society which speculates on the vagaries of racing, there exists a link between the two which cannot be disregarded.

Every week those of us who follow racing closely read in the sporting press the prophecies of eminent and very experienced gentlemen who earn a substantial income forecasting the probable winners of every important race.

Although a little healthy competition exists among them, their opinions never differ very widely. Their writings run into many columns describing the breeding, conformation and mannerisms of each of their special selections with a complete explanation of why over such and such a course with the going as it is at the particular moment, certain horses cannot be beaten by any of the other horses – all second-raters – in the race. After reading their contributions one will be perfectly satisfied that the bookmaking fraternity are greatly in need of pity, and one may even wonder why the owners of other horses entered in the race take the trouble to send them to the meeting. It is true that once in a blue moon a Santa Claus does turn up and highly reputable firms of turf accountants advertise the fact that they are another million pounds down as a result. But it is far more common to discover at the end of the race that one of the forecasters' unbeatable selections has come in fourth and that the first, second and third places are shared by horses which have entirely escaped their expert notice. That in itself may seem amazing, but there is something else even more so.

In the next issues of those same journals which have published such unfortunate prophecies, those same eminent and experienced gentlemen will carefully refrain from expressions of surprise but will contribute further reams in which they will extol the incomparable breeding, the immense speed and the wonderful staying powers of the ultimate winner, with favourable mention of the placed horses, and it is only those few unfortunates who have carefully preserved last week's edition who will have any inkling that their previous week's prophecies were a little wide of the mark.

The third amazing feature of racing is that should these same horses meet again over the same distance only a week or two later, their placings may be entirely different; the previous winner may come in nowhere and another outsider will win in a canter. This provides a further opportunity for the same gifted students of form to contribute a further article explaining why a horse carrying the blood of such an eminent sprinter or stayer as the case may be, could not fail to win on such an important occasion.

Those who have spent a lifetime reading the opinions of others best calculated to express them, studying form on one's own account and taking into consideration all the things which lead horses to gallop or to look upon racing with a jaundiced eye, are apt to end up by picking winners (often more successfully) with a pin, since it has become increasingly evident that if the same race could be run by the same horses and jockeys at fortnightly intervals the results would be entirely different on each occasion.

Thirty or forty years ago some of the most successful horses over hurdles were recruited from among those who raced only a mile on the flat, whether because that distance suited them or because they had not the ability to gallop any farther at top speed has never been decided. It is only occasionally that long-distance flat racers make successful hurdlers, because horses which stay on the flat are seldom possessed of the stamina that enables them to win a hurdle race, in which the horse must gallop fast for the whole distance and keep jumping without faltering or putting a foot wrong.

Why is it that horses capable of galloping long distances over hurdles do not go on to the flat and run away with races of a mile and a half or further? The reason is usually that modern race practice has turned the mile and a half flat race into a mile canter and a half-mile sprint and few steeplechasers can raise the necessary extra spurt at the end of the mile.

One may wonder sometimes what a really fast hurdler would do if it were galloped in a mile and a half flat race from the starting gate at really top speed. But horses, with a few exceptions (and these are mostly among jumpers), seldom gallop *away* from their fellows of their own free will at top speed.

Certain races over fences have shown quite recently that on occasion certain horses *do* show a marked inclination to lead from the start and maintain that lead. Most of them are 'pullers' which cannot be controlled, or ridden in any other fashion, and most of them, again, are unable to maintain the pace at the finish and are passed by the more sedate individuals. It is the *average* speed throughout the whole distance which has to be assessed in connection with winning or losing.

Hurdle races are run at such a speed from the start, nowadays, that horses tend to bunch together at the first few jumps, before certain horses take the lead. If these keep on their feet they stand a good chance of winning or being placed, but quite often a horse possessing stamina of a high order, takes up the running when the heat is turned on a few jumps from home and gaining position over every jump, runs in to win. On many racecourses a good deal depends upon the ability of the horse to gallop on the flat during the run home from the final jump. But, on the whole, hurdle races are run so fast that the eventual winner must gallop hard the whole distance without faltering or 'taking a breather' between jumps. The jumps must each be timed perfectly as a mistake may cause the loss of several lengths, even if it does not bring the horse down completely.

Many of our best horses over hurdles appear quite rough in coat and quite out of condition during a great part of the year, since a permanent state of fitness is unusual in man or horse and could only be maintained at the risk of a considerable shortening of the life span. The metabolism of the 'fit' athlete will be so stimulated that it burns up the tissues and gives rise to a depletion of the body's own nutritional requirements – in other words, any animal's digestive or metabolic processes cannot cope with excessive physical demands. The result is a cycle involving a resting state of the body, a building up of energy-producing compounds, a period in which the energy is dissipated, followed by a need for further rest.

Few flat racers during the winter months are easily recognisable as being the same horses which in their summer coats, muscled-up and brimming over with energy, are competing in classic events.

As for the hurdlers and 'chasers', in January they are either rough in coat or they are artificially advanced in condition by good feeding, warm boxes, grooming and rugging. By the beginning of March they are nearing their best and a month later going their hardest. The greater their fitness the fewer the falls.

The greatest horse race throughout the whole of the racing world, the Grand National, finds horses at their best unless they have been overworked during the earlier part of the season. It covers 4 miles 856 yards with thirty of the most awkward fences any horse will encounter during its racing life. (Plate 7.)

It is true, however, that many of these have been made easier by sloping their approaches and by other means, but they still require a lot of jumping and a great deal of stamina with a generous allowance of luck. During this century out of 1,816 starters, only 467 have completed the distance. The record for the race is probably that of Manifesto, who won the race on two occasions, was third three times, and was ninth at the age of 16. Only four favourites have won since 1900.

As I have written earlier, it is the human half of the combine that calls the tune and expects the horse to follow his (or her) lead.

The horse being by nature one individual in a herd lacks initiative and unless guided by the behaviour of the leader, or by that of the majority of its companions, is uncertain how best to behave. In a state of domestication, governed by the personality of its human trainer or rider, the average horse seeks guidance at all times and experiences a need to maintain a feeling of courage and confidence – something which it would lack if left all alone, dependent upon its own initiative.

So long as the rider is confident, capable and courageous, so long will the horse be with him, or her, in body and spirit, but the moment the rider loses confidence the horse will become brightened and undecided regarding its own intentions.

A good jockey will nurse his horse until the moment of truth. He will then call upon it with his mind and his will, stimulate it by touch, and by his own outpouring of energy induce it to make a supreme effort, to pour forth its last ounce of strength.

If the jockey succeeds, his mount will respond readily, if it is still capable of so doing. If the jockey is himself exhausted, or if he is unable to infuse the necessary degree of urge into the mind of his horse, he will fail to raise within it the degree of enthusiasm necessary to produce a maximum effort, and in such a case it will be the jockey, not the horse, that fails.

This is the principle which lies behind all racing and indeed behind all forms of sport or work in which the horse is ever engaged. But racing, like all other exciting occupations, is conditioned by the element of chance – by the luck of the game – and there is never any guarantee that the best horse ridden by the best jockey will be first past the post. Were it not so, racing would be a humdrum affair, devoid of interest.

Horses get left at the starting gate or get away badly, they become badly placed, crowded in or crowded out, held up or brought down by fallen horses, hampered by wind and rain, not least, by mud.

One should stop and speculate, when one sees a lot of horses parading before a race, cantering along to the starting place and lining-up for the start, as to what is really going on within the horse's mind.

Does the horse 'wonder' what is about to happen? From previous experience it may remember that the routine is similar to that which has preceded other gallops in company with a number of horses – all strangers. It might not be right to say that the horses realises that the gallop in such company is in any sense a 'race', since it has no understanding of what goes on in the human mind and no knowledge that, wherever it may be placed during the gallop that will follow, its head must be in front of every other horse's head, when it reaches a spot exactly a mile, or perhaps five furlongs, from the starting gate. As I have pointed out already, none of the competitors will have any idea of where this spot may be, since nobody has taught it that a certain object – 'the winning post' – indicates the termination of the gallop, or that this post has any special significance.

The one thing that very few horses want to do naturally is to take the lead. This does not imply that by the right kind of psychological training a young horse could not be conditioned into taking the lead and, in fact, this habit can easily be instilled into a young horse – but seldom is.

A great many years ago the author, then a young man, was 'seeing practice' with an experienced veterinary surgeon regarded as one of the successful trainers of his day, although he handled comparatively few horses. His method was to send out a string of horses for walking exercise. Riding on his cob alongside he would blow a whistle at intervals of one to three minutes. This would be the signal for the last horse in the string to canter forward and take the lead. After an hour of this, every horse had experience of racing to the front on command. Presently the exercise would be repeated at a canter, with the result that no horse ever remained content with hanging at the rear end of the line or even in the centre of the group. This gentleman used to declare that, when racing, any one of his horses could be depended upon to make a determined effort to go to the front whenever called upon to do so.

The main drawback to encouraging horses to take the lead is that, as modern races are run, very few jockeys are at all anxious that their mounts *should* take the lead, until that critical second arrives when all the heat is turned on and at that moment the ability to take the lead – at the exact spot on the course known only to the jockey – is the one thing that can ensure success.

When we think of the reasons – apart from the influence of the rider – which may persuade horses to gallop at a fast rate, we must always remember that buried deep in the mentality of every horse lies what is known as the 'escape reaction'. In wild life this was coupled with a 'distance reaction', which refers to the closeness to which any animal will permit another to approach, before its urge to escape assumes command.

When a horse, even today in its domesticated, protected state, is threatened by anything that may give rise to suspicion, fear, or to that odd indescribable feeling of being 'muddled-up' so common today among all kinds of living creatures, its behaviour terminates, usually quite suddenly, in a manifestation of the 'escape reaction'. In other words, the animal turns tail and bolts. Its one thought – if we can permit the horse to think in this way – is that it must take the bit between its teeth, if there is one in the mouth endeavouring to exert control, and gallop madly in any direction, away from the dreaded spot and continue to gallop, either until it reaches a place of safety, or, maybe, until it stops from sheer exhaustion.

As I pointed out earlier, this escape reaction is one of the most primitive urges, one that in primeval days may have been a help towards survival, but is less suited to an age when marauding animals are almost extinct and fast traffic leaves little space for mad gallops. This does not apply only to the horse, for it is a form of response which even the civilised human being has failed to banish from his own complex mentality.

In the horse the reaction lies nearer the surface. The impulse is more overpowering than in many other animals less highly strung, and the horse that runs away is merely obeying an impulse too strong to resist. It has lost confidence in its own ability to cope with an existing situation and, if mounted, has also lost faith in the ability of its rider to afford it protection.

The escape reaction is, of course, not confined to horses. It is present in most animals and is very obvious among herds of game and even among creatures as powerful as elephants, and in those as small and weak as rodents.

It seems possible that racing and the escape reaction may be closely associated in the mind of the horse. There is a period of excitement in the paddock and when horses are collected at the starting gate. At the start horses are urged forward and the general rush begins, comparable with what used to happen when a collection of horses made their escape from a marauding animal endeavouring to spring upon the slowest or upon the lame one in their midst. But the instinct of the horse was only to gallop out of range of the marauder and this need not be more perhaps than a few hundred yards. When this point is reached the rider takes command and urges the horse to maintain the gallop. By his own excitement he may prolong the desire of the horse to escape. But once away from all the hullabaloo of the start, the shouts of the jockeys and the general state of excitement, the impulse to gallop at high speed begins to weaken, and it can only be maintained through the contact made with the rider and the inspiration derived from him.

But, once again, the natural instinct of the horse is to gallop somewhere in the *midst* of the flock. Only the ordained leader normally goes in front, and yet the whole art of racing is centred upon getting the nose of one's own mount at least a fraction of an inch *in front of* every other nose at an exact moment during the race. (Plate 8.)

And, do not forget, this has to be eventually achieved at a given moment – at the passing of the winning post – and the horse has no knowledge of its existence.

One may wonder whether, in these circumstances, every horse is really producing its best effort, or if it could put on an

extra bit of speed at the appropriate moment if it were aware
of the purpose of the race.

Herein, of course, lies all the joy, the excitement and the
uncertainty of racing.

This would seem to be a suitable moment to look carefully at
the other side of the picture and endeavour to imagine the kind
of impression all this enforced galloping about, running mad
races over obstacles, or careering at breakneck speed on the
flat, conveys to the mind of the horse.

How, for instance, does a horse react mentally to the form of
human behaviour which induces a number of mounted men
to chase persistently at top speed a small roll of wood, up and
down a limited area of ground, in an effort to hit it with a
stick?

It is fortunate, perhaps, that the mentality of the horse
renders it utterly incapable of assessing that of its human
colleagues. Were it otherwise, since the human and equine
sense of values must be so different, the horse might form the
opinion that men – and even women – were utterly insane and
that there was no method in their particular form of mad-
ness.

In addition, fortunately in some instances, unfortunately
in others, the horse can have no conception of the purpose of
its rider other than that it is required to gallop, jump, or come
to a standstill on command. It has no knowledge of its rider's
ultimate aim or what the sum total of its activities are designed
to accomplish.

A horse can possess little or no understanding of *why* it
should be necessary to gallop from two to four miles over
difficult jumping country at top speed that strains its heart
and lungs, when there appears to be no trace of any pursuing
enemy close upon its tail, nor can it see the necessity for such
exertion apart from the fact that a number of other horses,
often strangers quite unknown to it, are behaving in precisely
the same way.

Similarly, although a pony may be sufficiently irresponsible
and even high-spirited to enjoy, within certain limits, a romp
around a gymkhana field in company with others of its kind, it

can have no understanding of why it should be necessary to gallop madly and repeatedly to some unspecified spot only a short distance away, come to a sudden stop while its owner dismounts and reaches for something on the ground and re-mounts; and then gallop the length of the field until the owner makes contact with a sack hung upon a pole, the whole being expedited by the shouts of its juvenile rider and by the repeated kicks which it receives in its ribs from the heels of a pair of riding boots.

Potatoes, the pony might argue, may be quite nice to munch in a spare moment, but why all this urgent need to gather them in such a ridiculous manner?

We have always to bear constantly in mind that only the human members of this partnership between the horses and their riders have the least idea as to why it is necessary for both of them to behave in such an odd fashion, and why any self-respecting horse or pony should be compelled to do so, or why they should be expected to indulge in antics which for them can have little or no meaning.

But, their youthful riders will say, the ponies enjoy it. It is true that they may do so provided they are treated with con-sideration and kindness, but only as the result of excitement induced by the enthusiasm of their riders; certainly not because they understand or appreciate the purpose of the whole per-formance.

Show jumping, which I have mentioned earlier, comes into a rather different category since the horse has been trained, sometimes for years, to jump over a series of obstacles arranged in a field, on almost every occasion it is taken out of the stable. Although it becomes conditioned to this pattern of behaviour, it still has no understanding of why jumping ability should be a matter of such great importance. It develops ability, firstly because it is persuaded by its rider to jump, and secondly, because it learns from experience that, once having consented to do so, bumping its cannons and fetlocks against wooden rails or bricks can be both painful and upsetting in every sense of the word; even more so when every mistake happens to be followed by a cut from the whip. The horse learns that the easiest solution is to endeavour to clear every jump to its rider's satisfaction.

Horses, as I have mentioned earlier, seldom receive any rewards for success whatever they may receive in case of failure, but then again, unlike dogs, horses rarely associate the receipt of a pat, or even a lump of sugar, with the accomplishment of a clear round.

It would seem, therefore, that the horse in humouring its rider to an extent which permits the achievement of his, or her, particular aims, the nature of which the horse is entirely unaware, displays a degree of unselfish co-operative endeavour which would be regarded as sufficiently meritorious in human society to cause its perpetrator to be numbered among the saints.

We are presuming, of course, that the co-operation is entirely voluntary and not brought into being by ill-treatment and by cruel use of the whip and spur. When it is obtained by such means, it is reasonable to suppose that the mind of the horse must become even more muddled than when it gives its help voluntarily and feels that its co-operation pleases its rider. It is no wonder that a bad rider, or one lacking understanding of the mentality or feelings of the horse, should ruin the animal's temperament and destroy all desire on its part to co-operate in a type of behaviour which is attended by suffering and probably by fear. (Plate 6.)

It is true that some horses respond to applause provided by a human gathering. They are not possessed of the same sense of understanding as dogs are in this respect, since many performing dogs await applause and are as proud to receive it as are human actors. It is a fact, however, that many horses, in a jumping competition especially, give some indications that they are sensitive to this expression of human emotions, though whether the flicking of the tail and tendency sometimes to buck is due to understanding or merely to excitement caused by the extra volume of sound, is never quite clear.

I have driven horses in the show-ring which, when passing the grandstand, would respond to applause by an exaggeration of their prevailing type of action, usually with the unfortunate result that they broke step and momentarily went off balance and the whole effect was ruined.

It is essential to regard the behaviour of the horse as one should that of all animals, with a complete absence of anthropomorphism. In other words, one must never attribute to the animal any of the qualities which one might desire to see it possess, purely on sentimental grounds, without any concrete evidence to justify one's belief. One is apt, because some animals are so closely associated with their owners, to compare favourably some of their behaviour with that which would be expected in similar circumstances from a reasoning human being. Admitting that some animals possess considerably greater intelligence than others of their species, it would be quite wrong to attribute human behaviour and that of other animals to the same causes since, while our own brains enable us to think and reason correctly or incorrectly, the mentality of the horse does not permit it to solve problems, although some of its natural responses to everyday stimuli may occasionally give the impression that it can do so.

The horse that learns to draw back the bolt of its loose-box door with its lips, even when this involves considerable ingenuity, is undoubtedly displaying intelligence, but in all probability the solution of the problem was originally accidental, though the horse remembers how to repeat the operation. Quite a lot of human knowledge is acquired in the same way.

It may be that some of the other tricks horses learn are acquired in similar fashion, but the nearest approach to intelligence I have observed was displayed by a farm mare whose hind fetlock had become entangled in a length of barbed wire at the bottom of a fence. In this case the mare seemed to consider the problem, then placed her free foot on the wire, pressed it down and released her other foot.

In the mind of the animal including that of the horse, there is no question whether certain things should or should not be done. The sole criterion is whether any particular type of behaviour increases, or lessens, the animal's chances of survival.

There is a possibility that the horse realises sooner or later that its board and lodging depend upon the goodwill of its owner and that it is good policy to gratify his or her whims. Whether we should concede this much is debatable, but, in this instance, we are justified in assuming that most horses are willing, after a course of education, to carry out patterns of behaviour entirely opposed to their own natural instincts, solely to please an owner whose motives are quite beyond the horse's comprehension.

With that in mind, it behoves us to treat the horse with the degree of consideration, and accord to it the gratitude, it deserves.

Index

Index